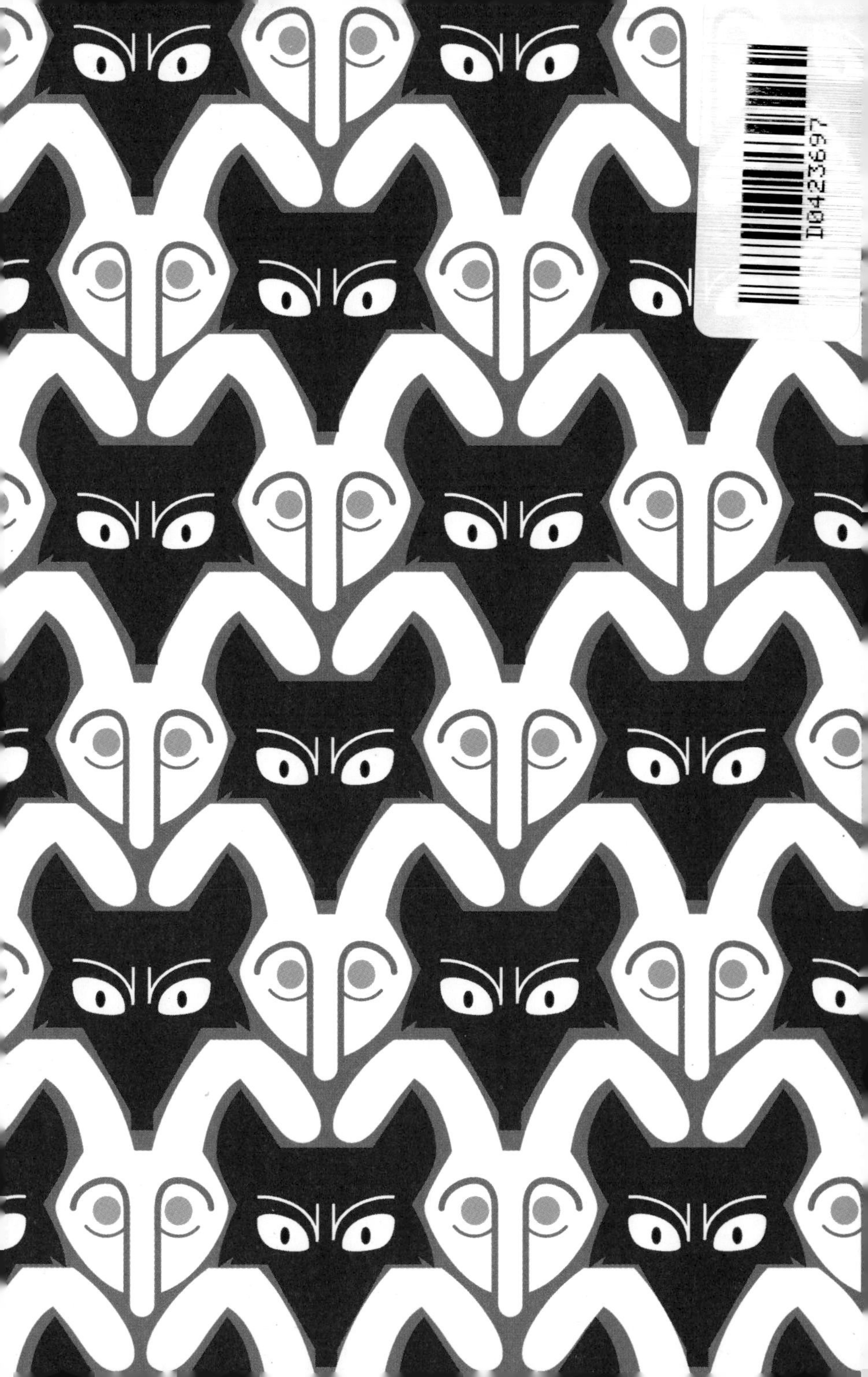

Thanks,
Diane!

Andy Hartzell

FOX BUNNY FUNNY

by Andy Hartzell

TOP SHELF PRODUCTIONS
ATLANTA/PORTLAND

Published by Top Shelf Productions,
PO Box 1282, Marietta, GA 30061-1282, USA.
Publishers: Brett Warnock and Chris Staros.

Visit our online catalog at www.topshelfcomix.com.

First Printing, June 2007. Printed in Canada.

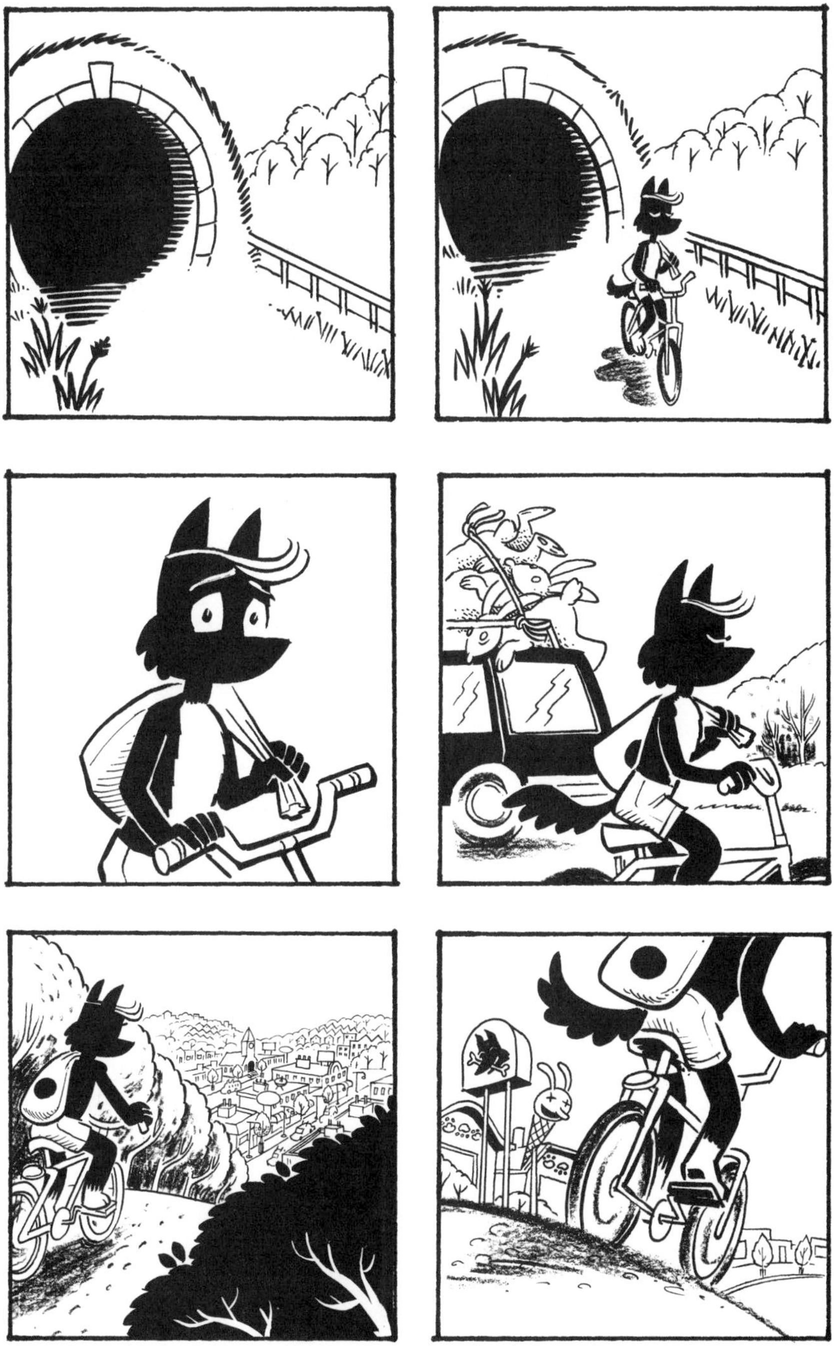

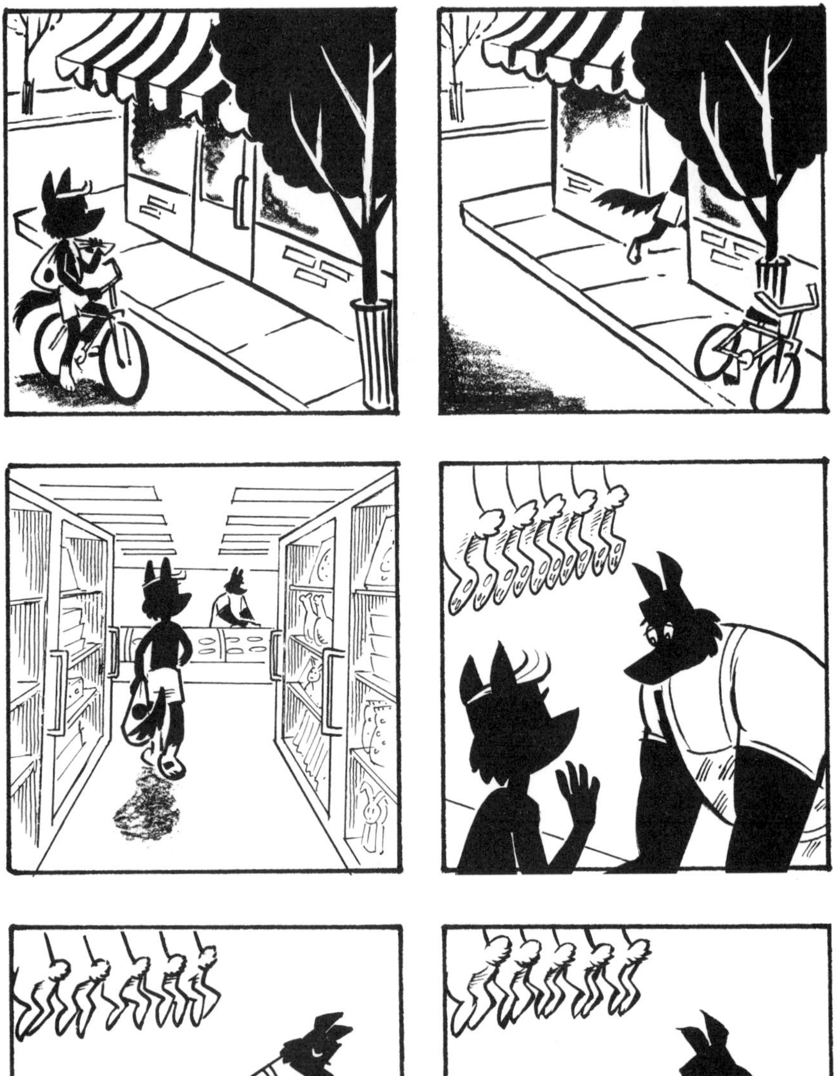

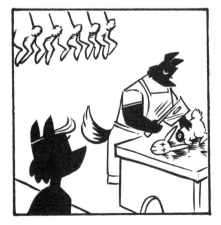

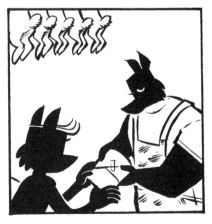

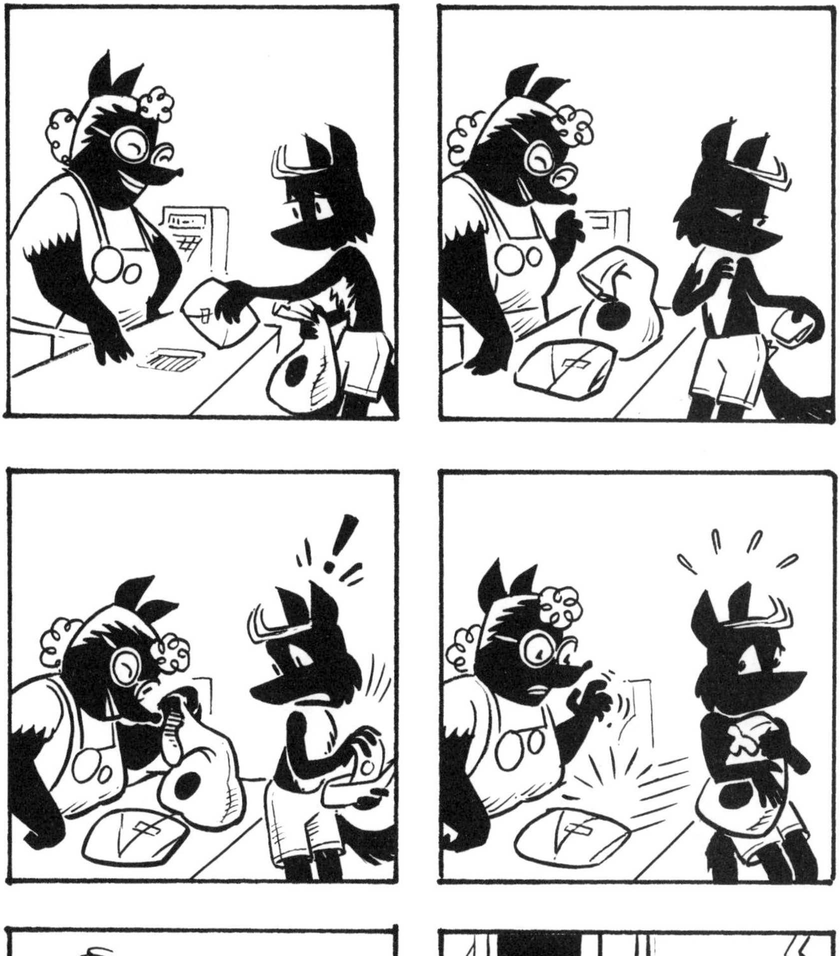

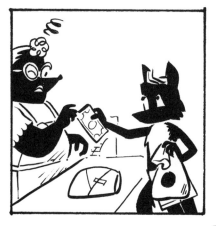

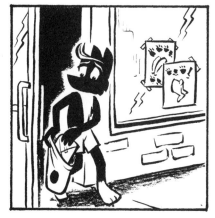

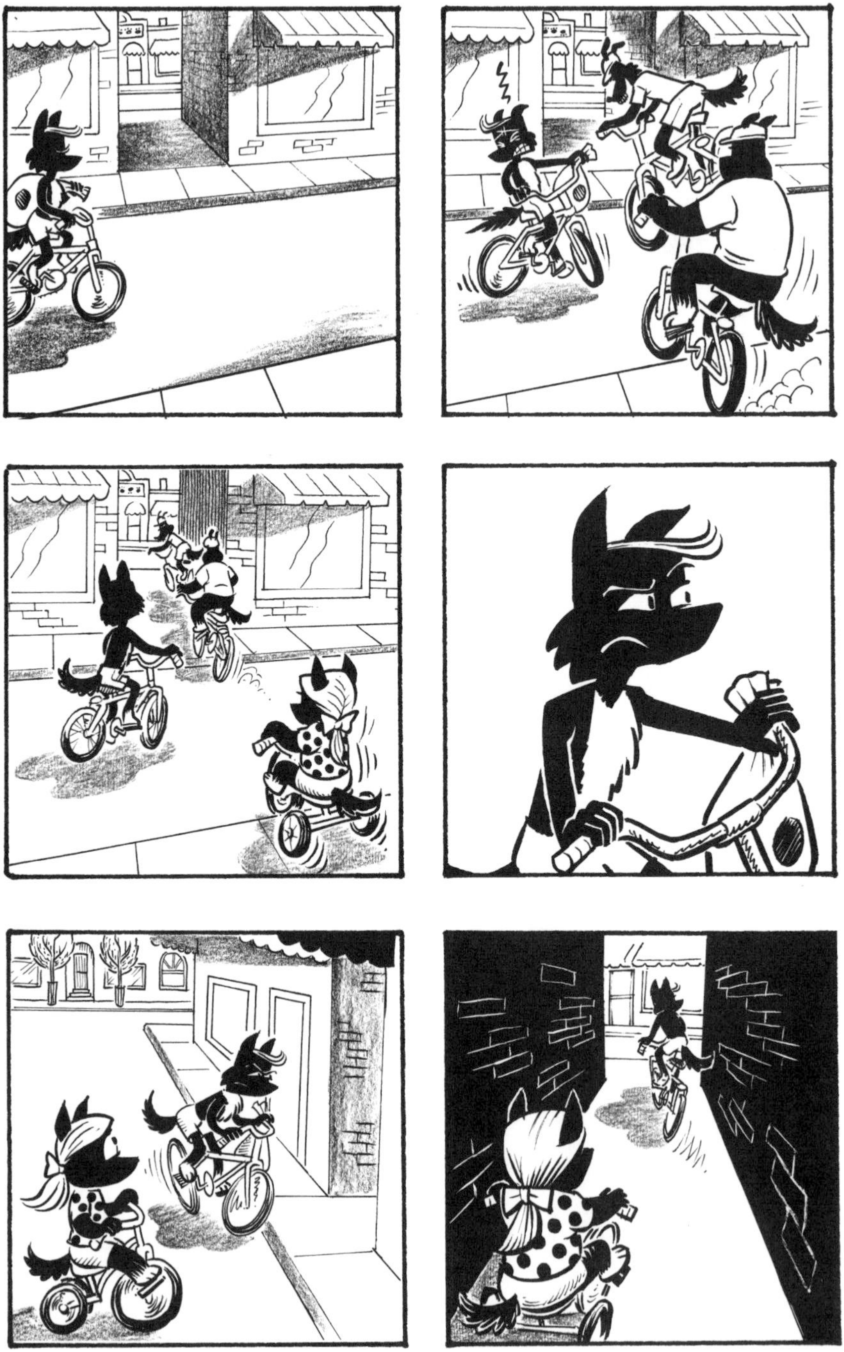

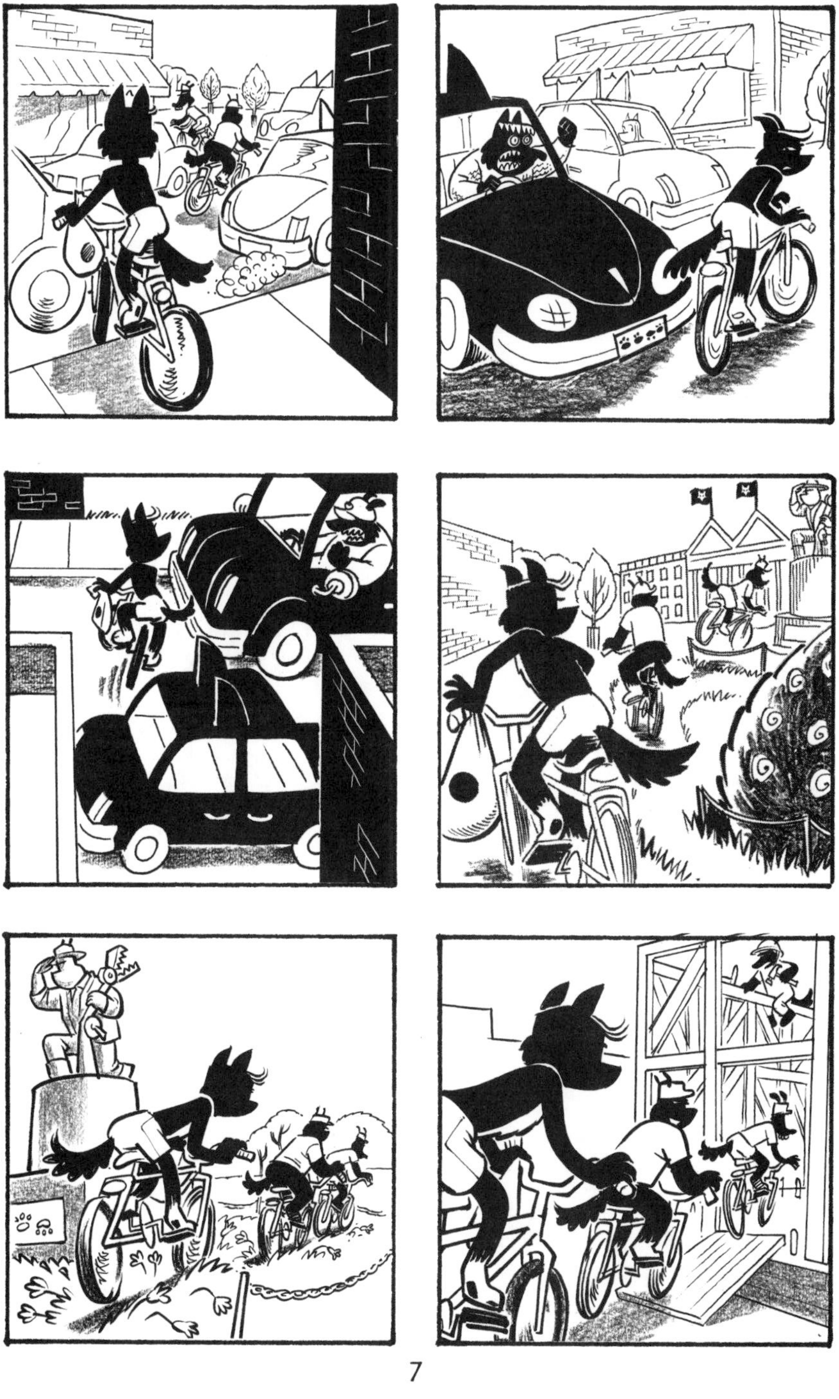

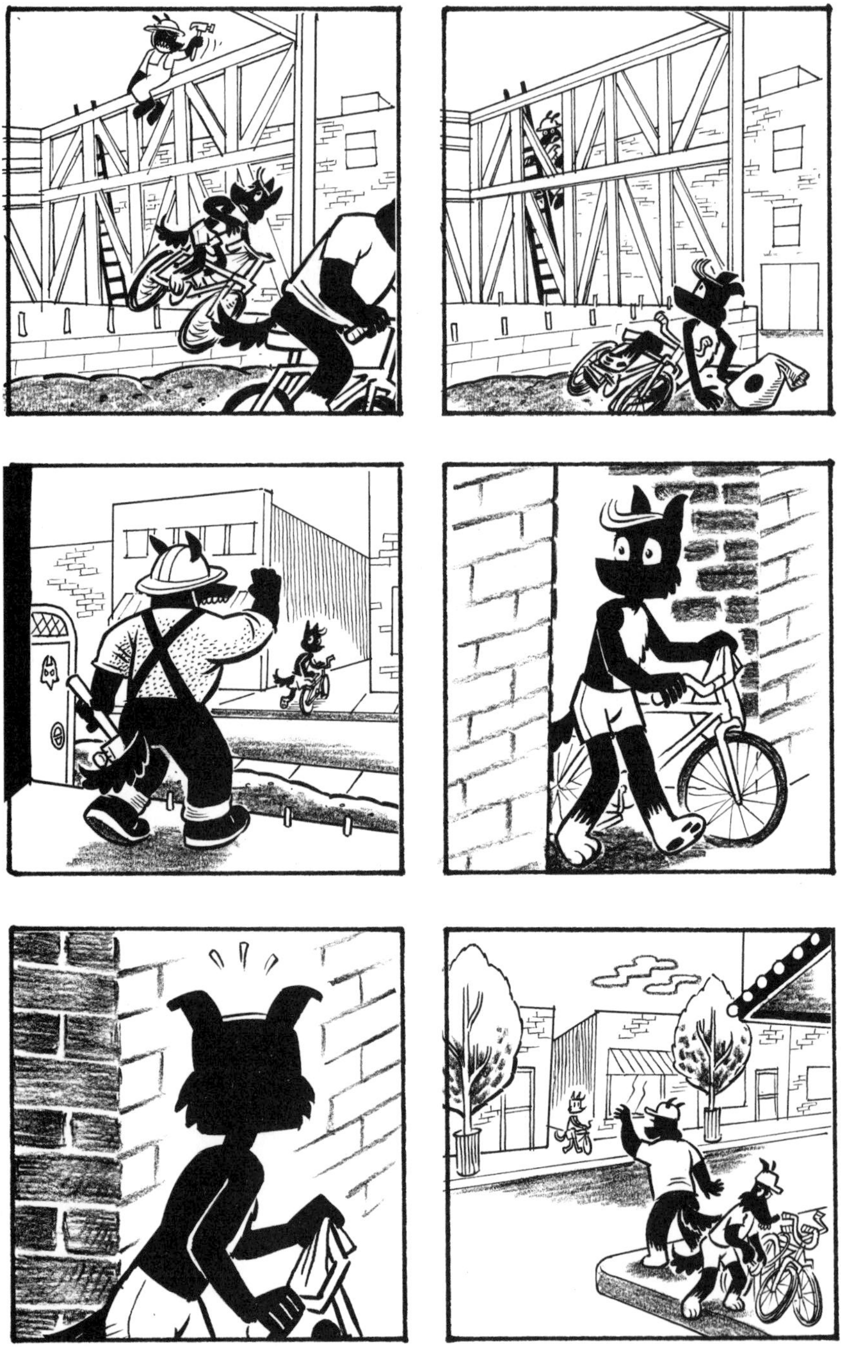

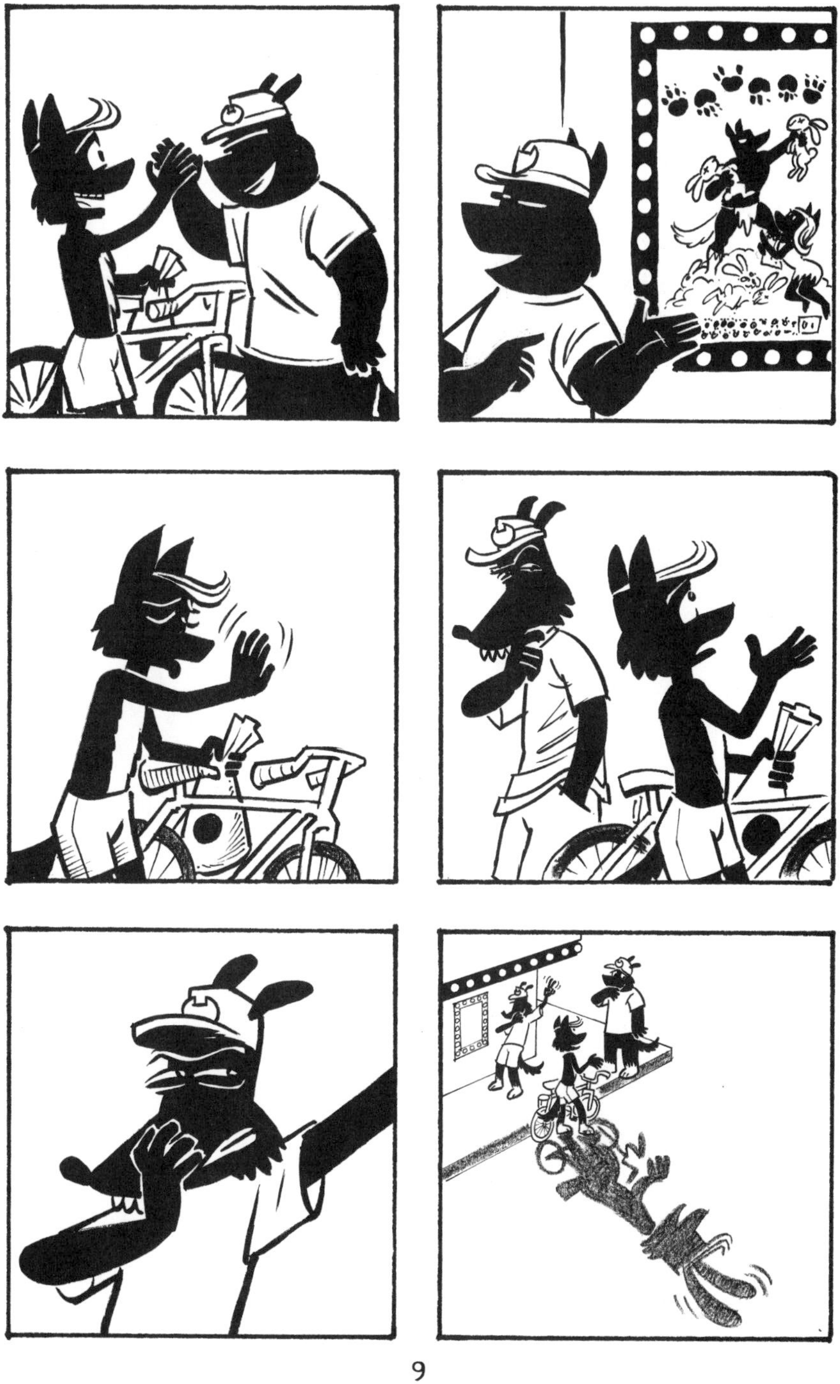

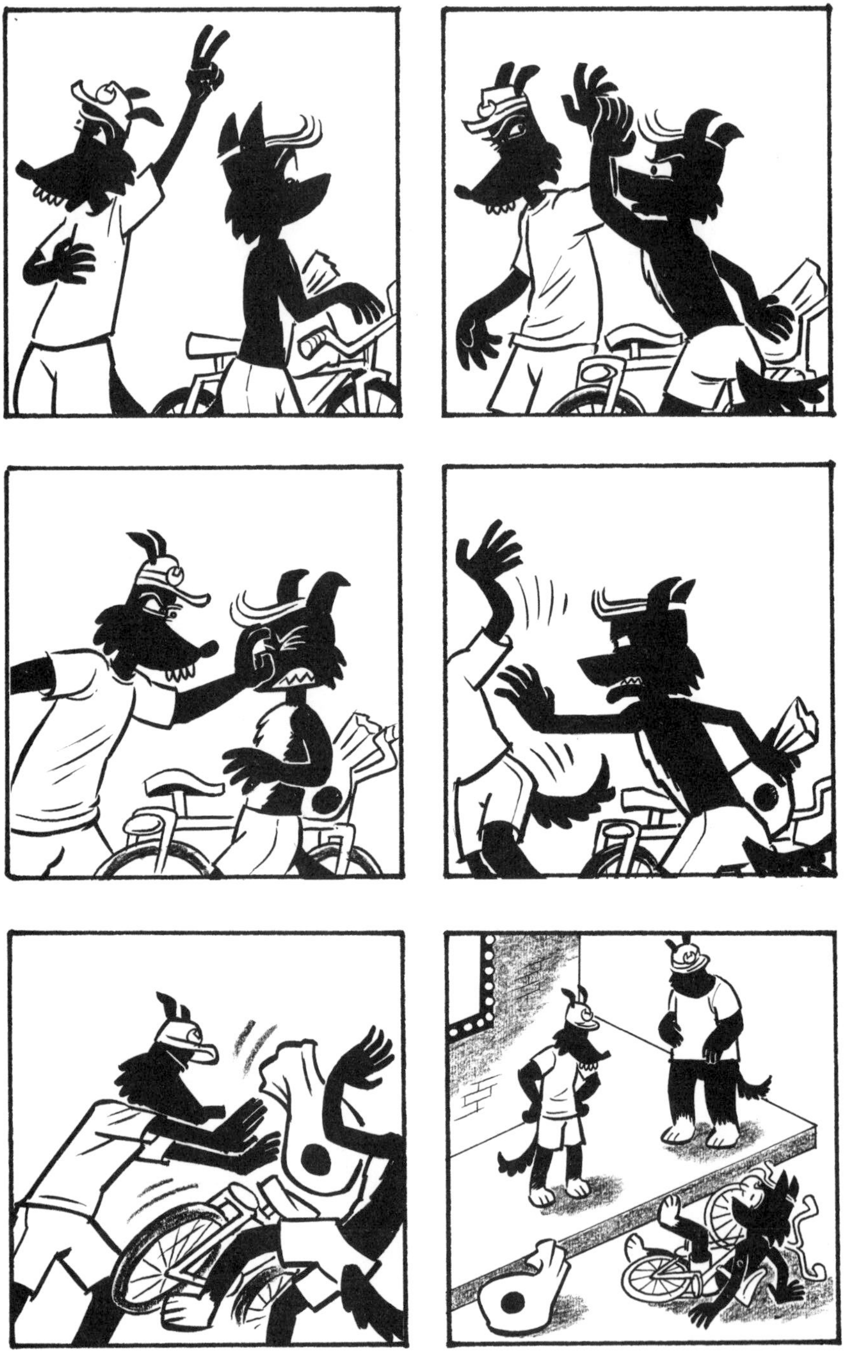

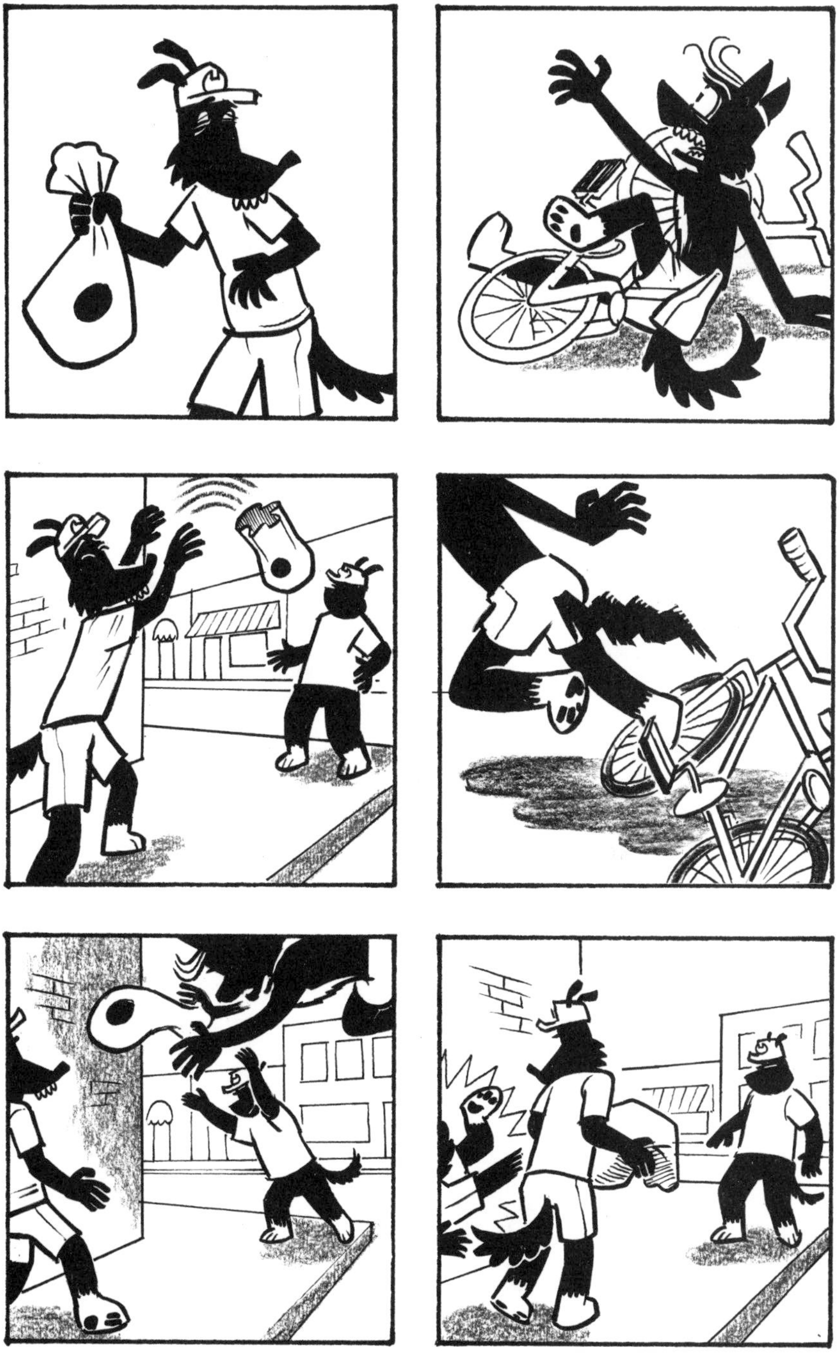

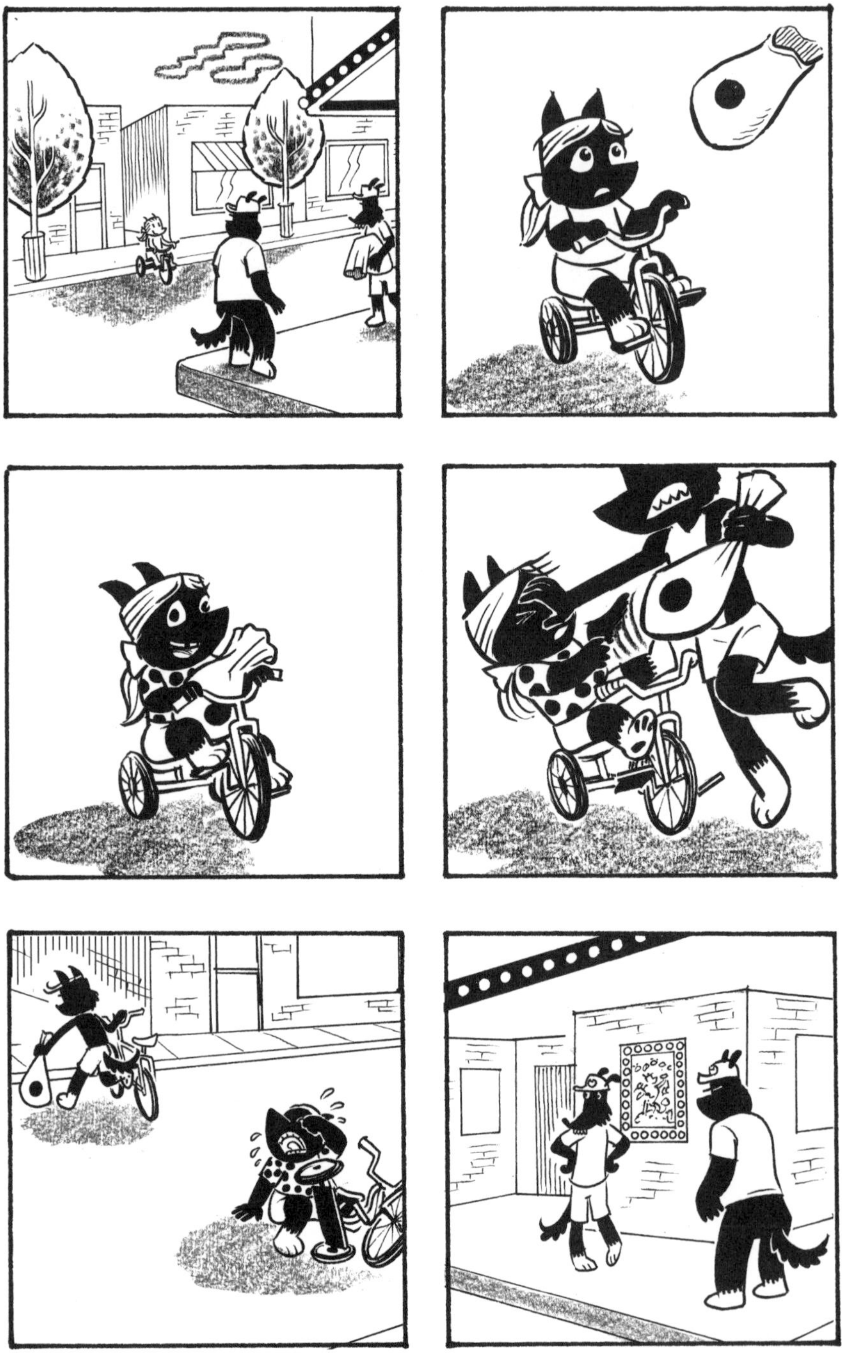

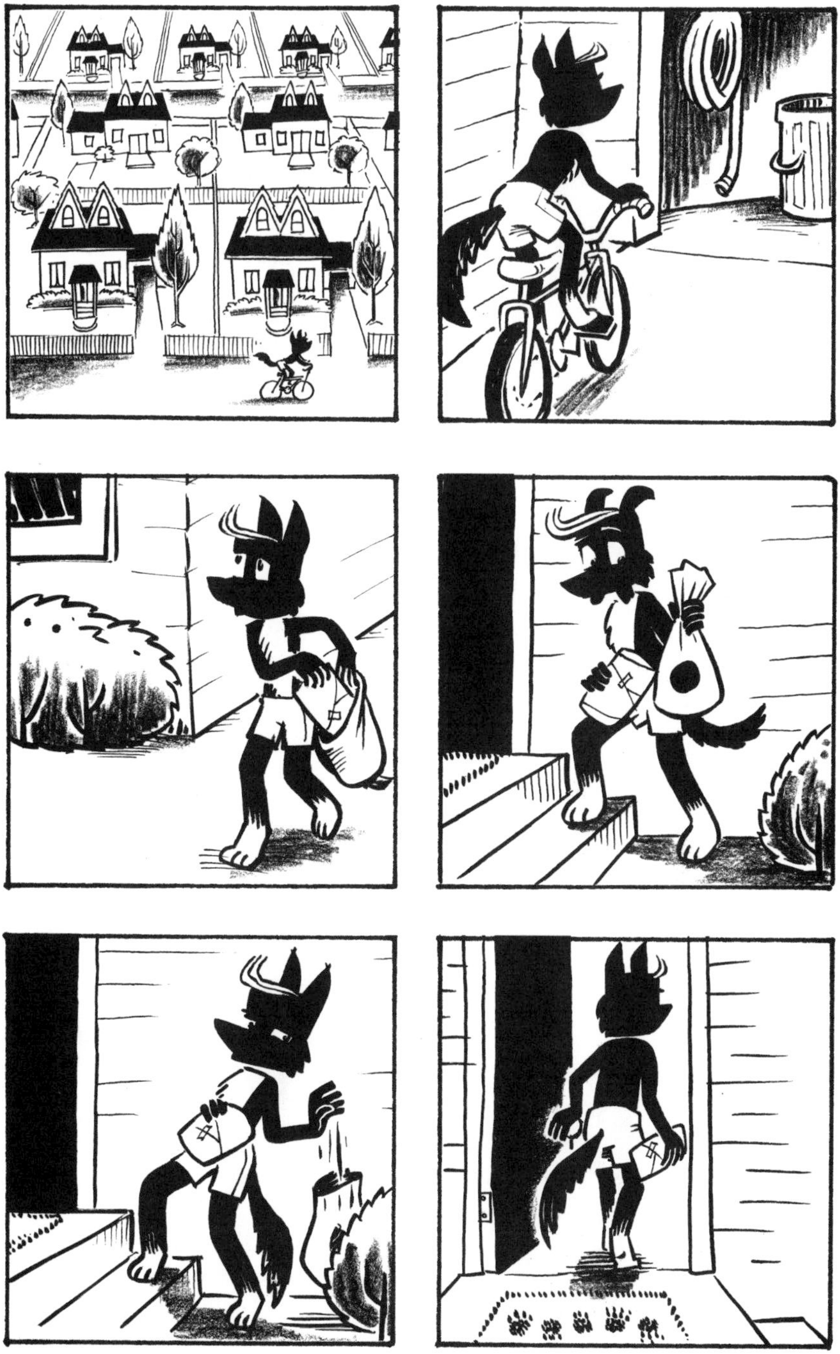

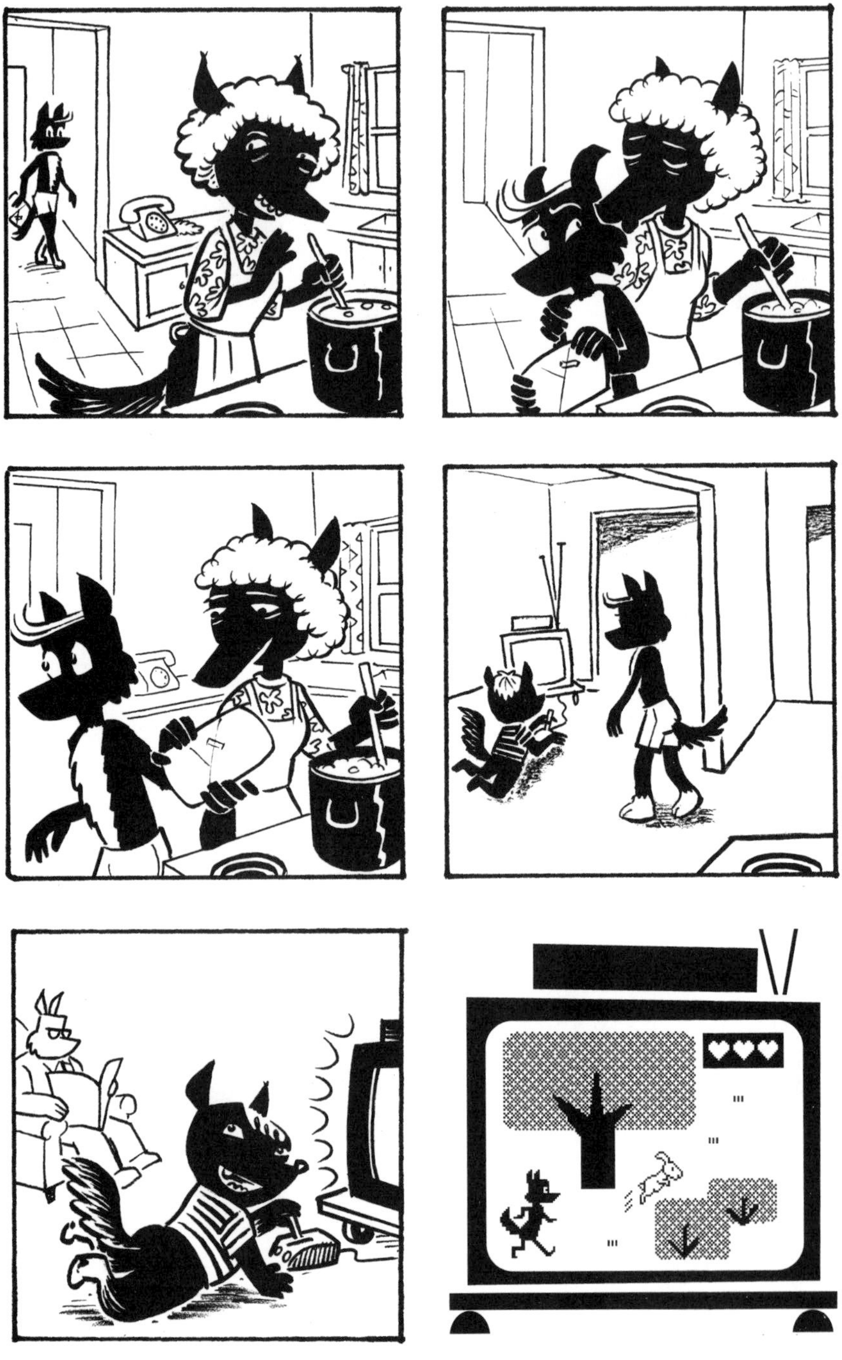

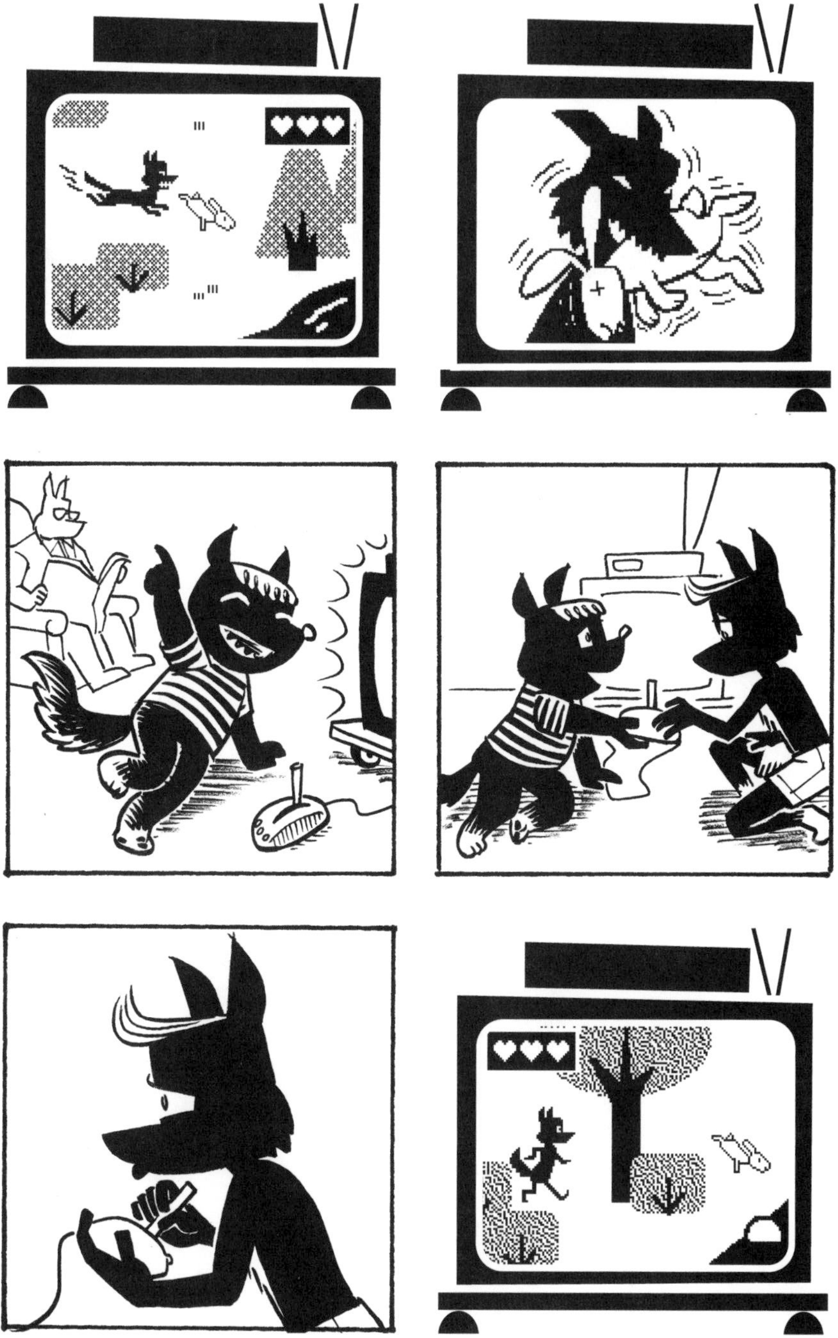

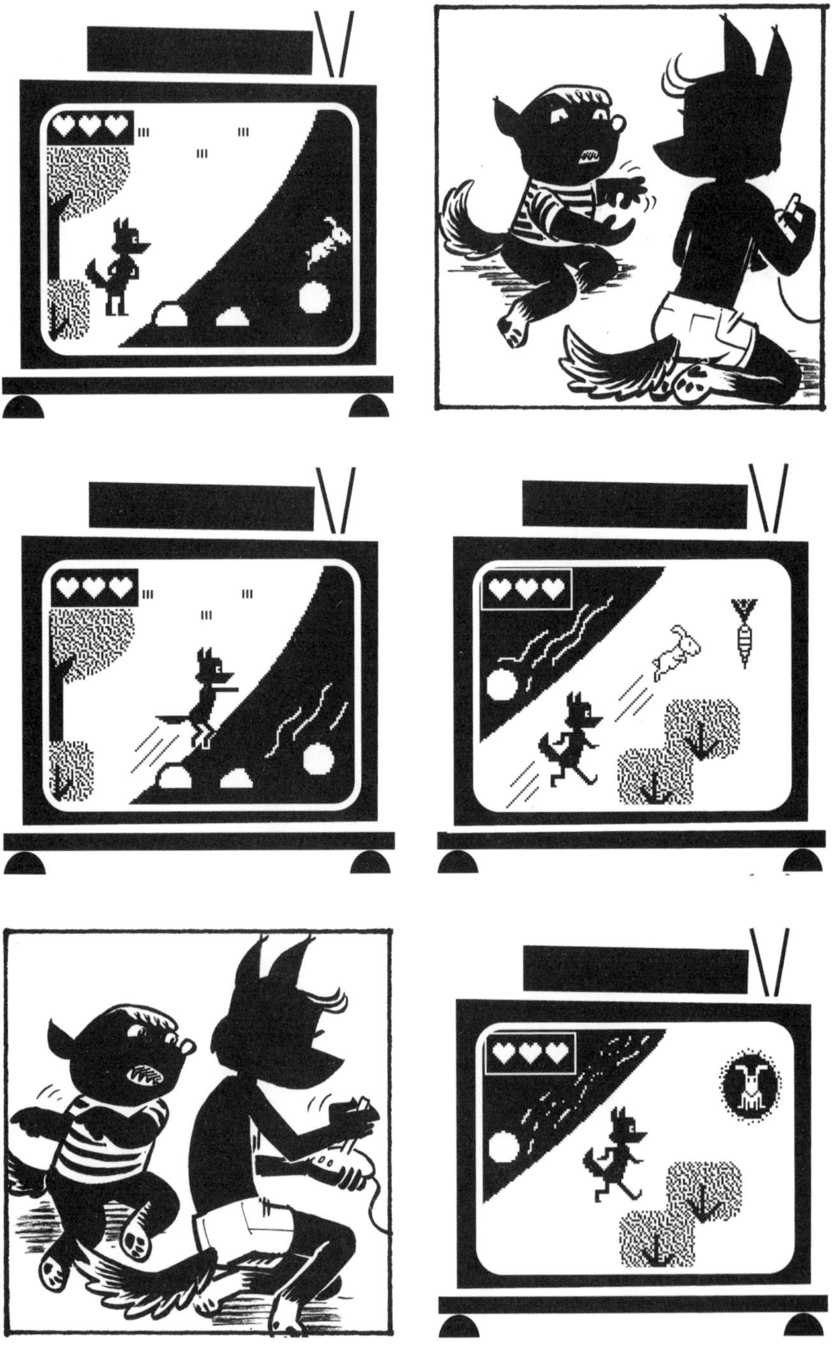

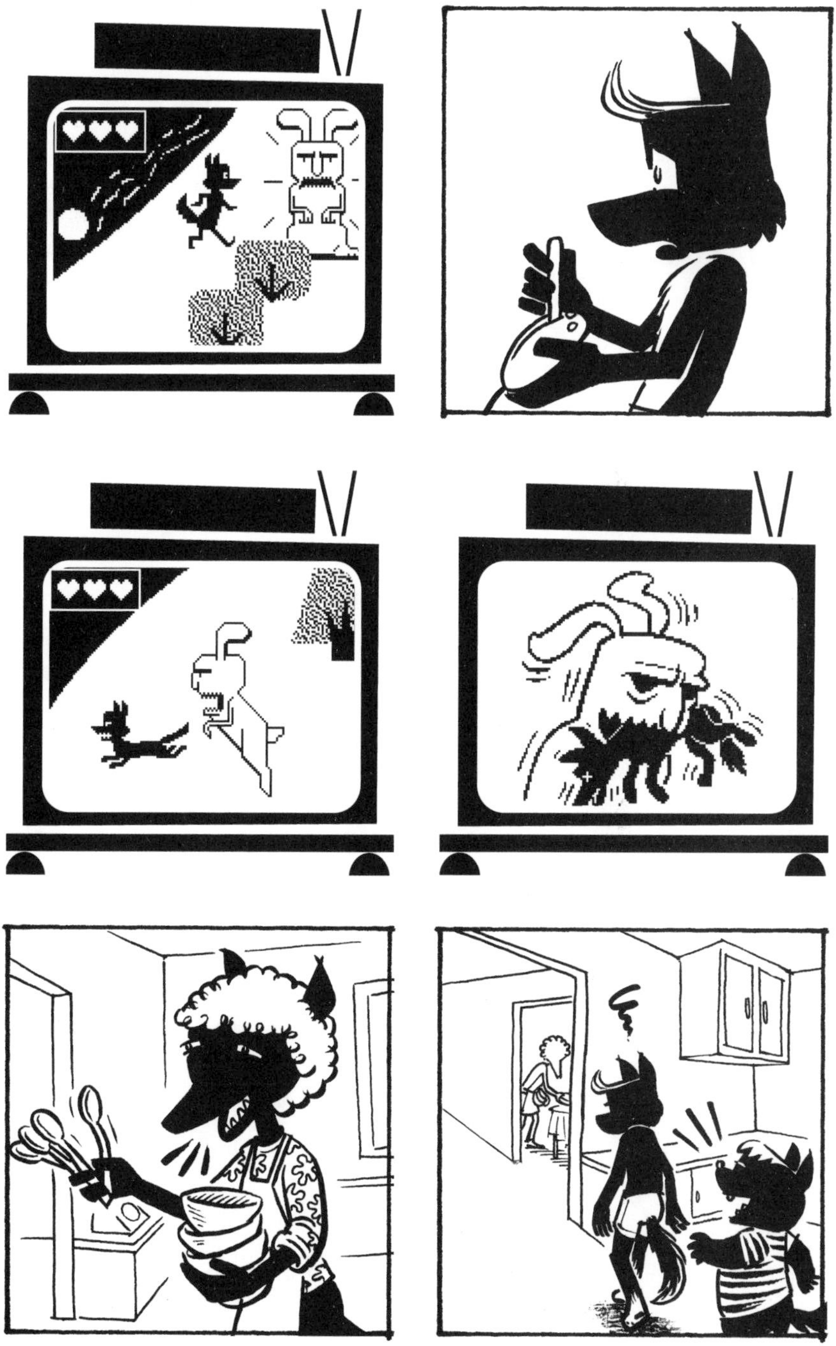

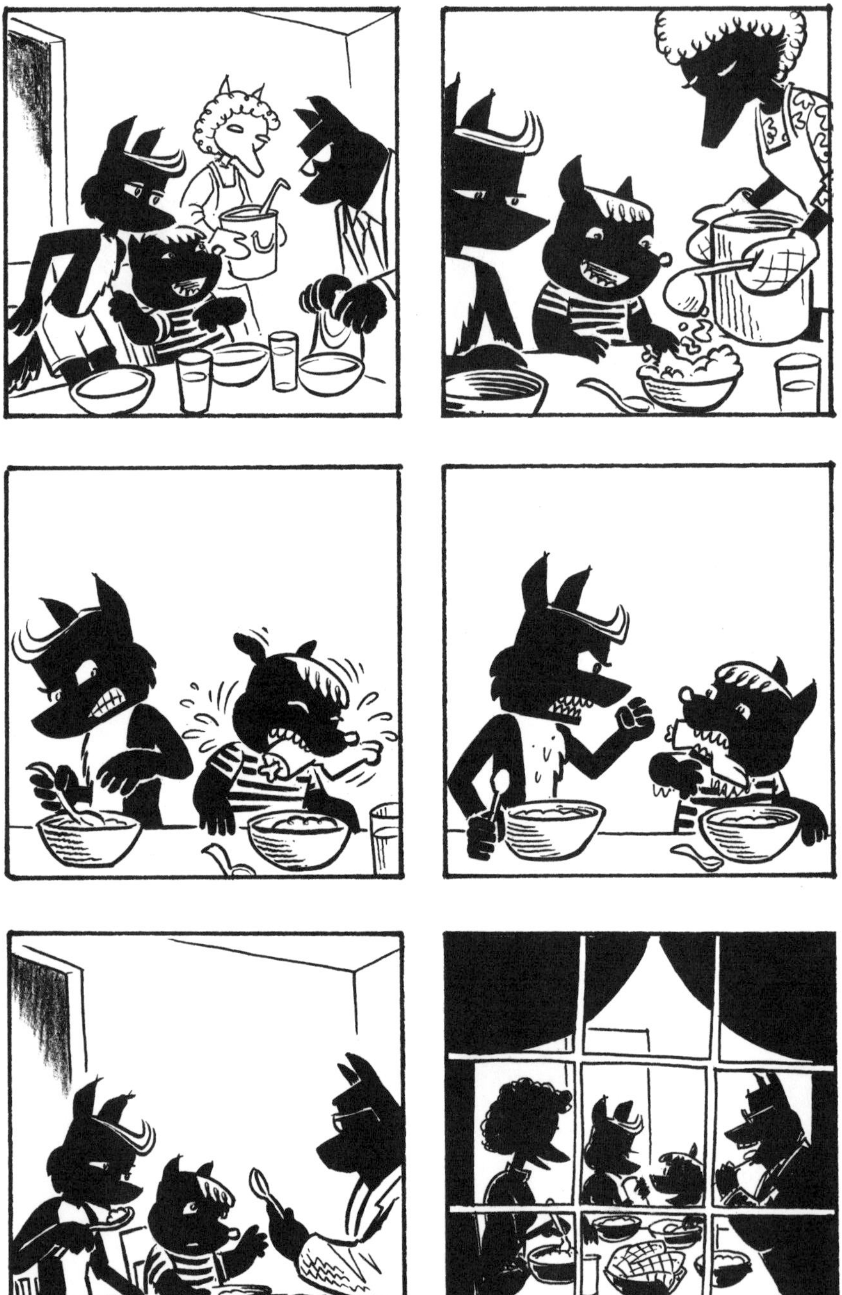

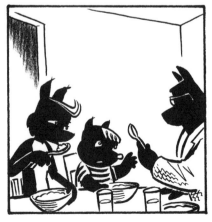

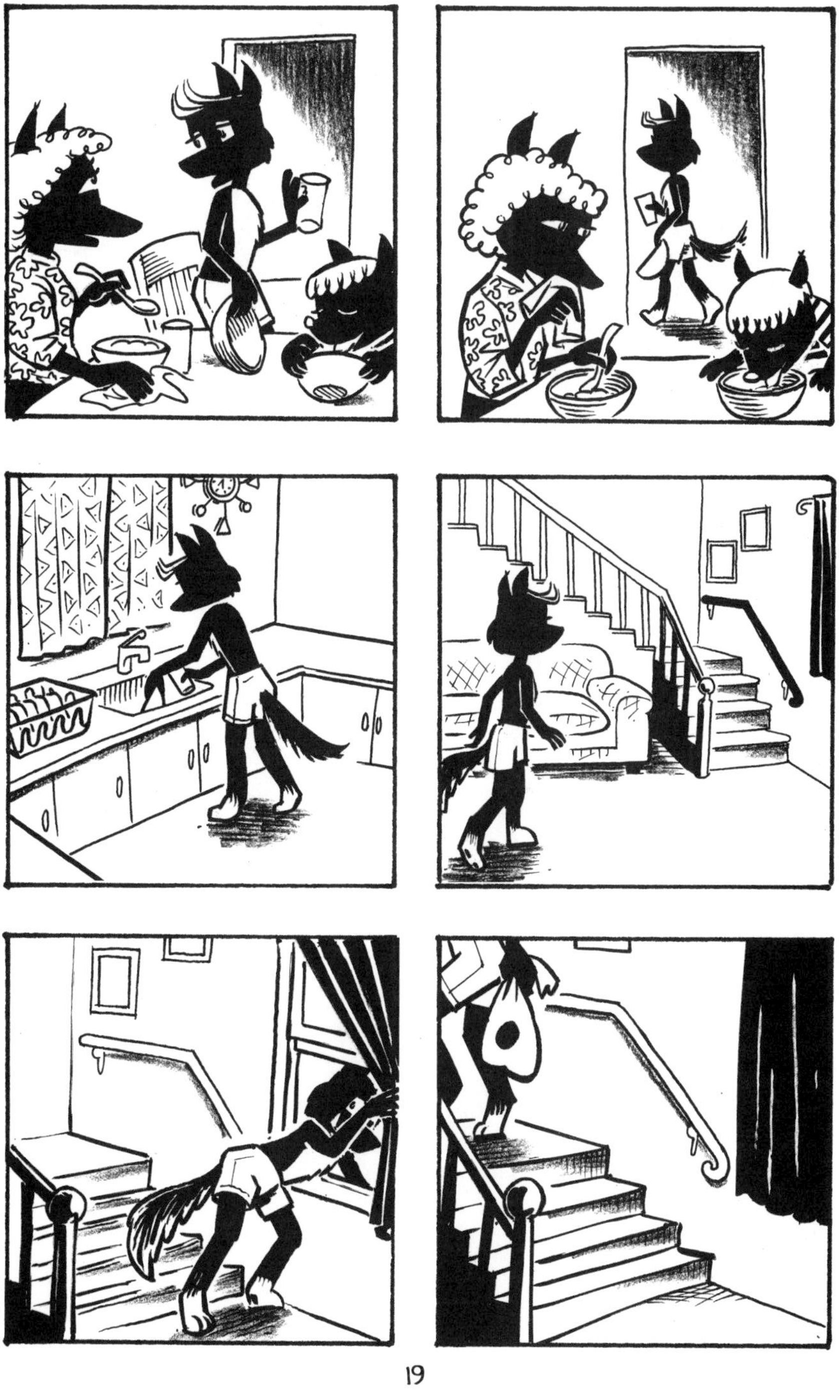

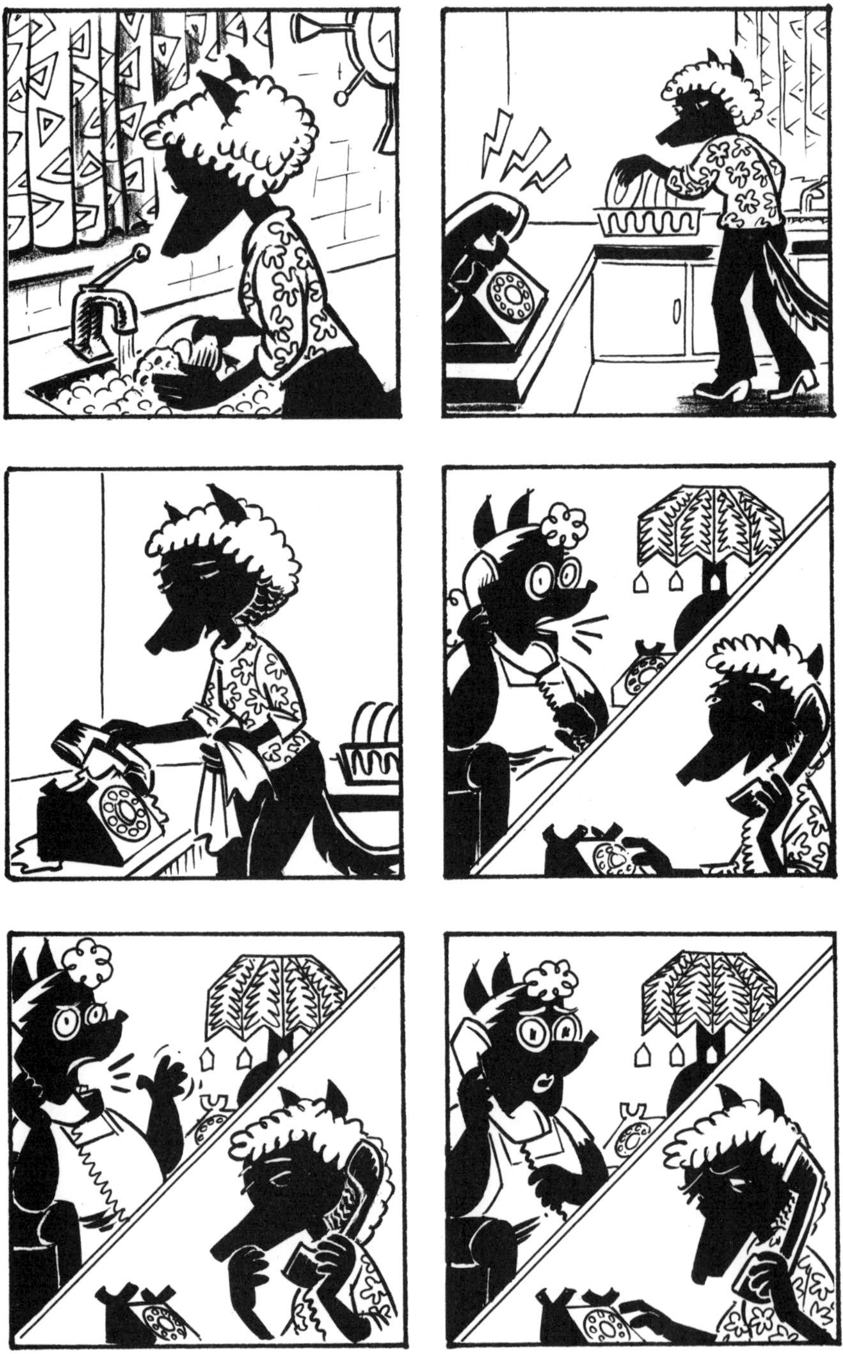

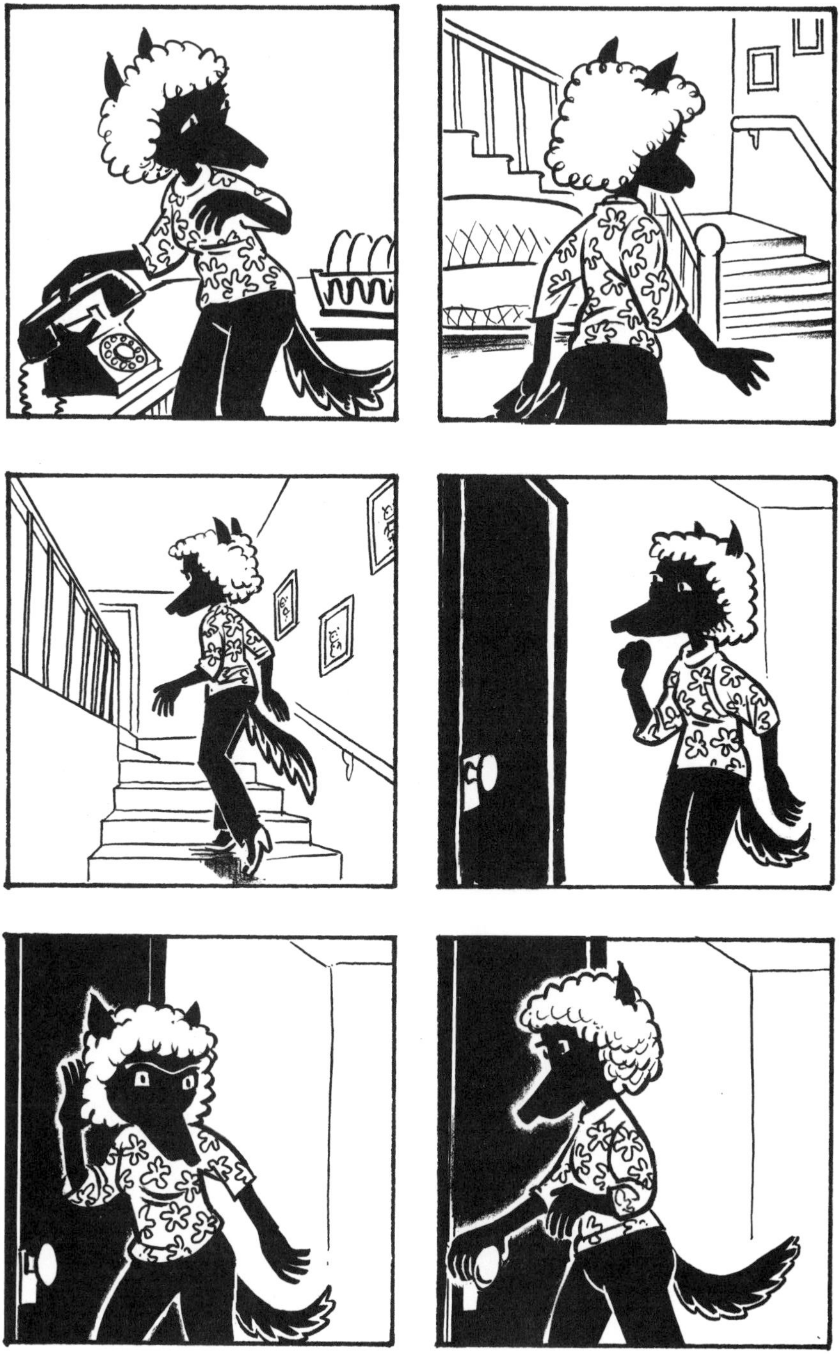

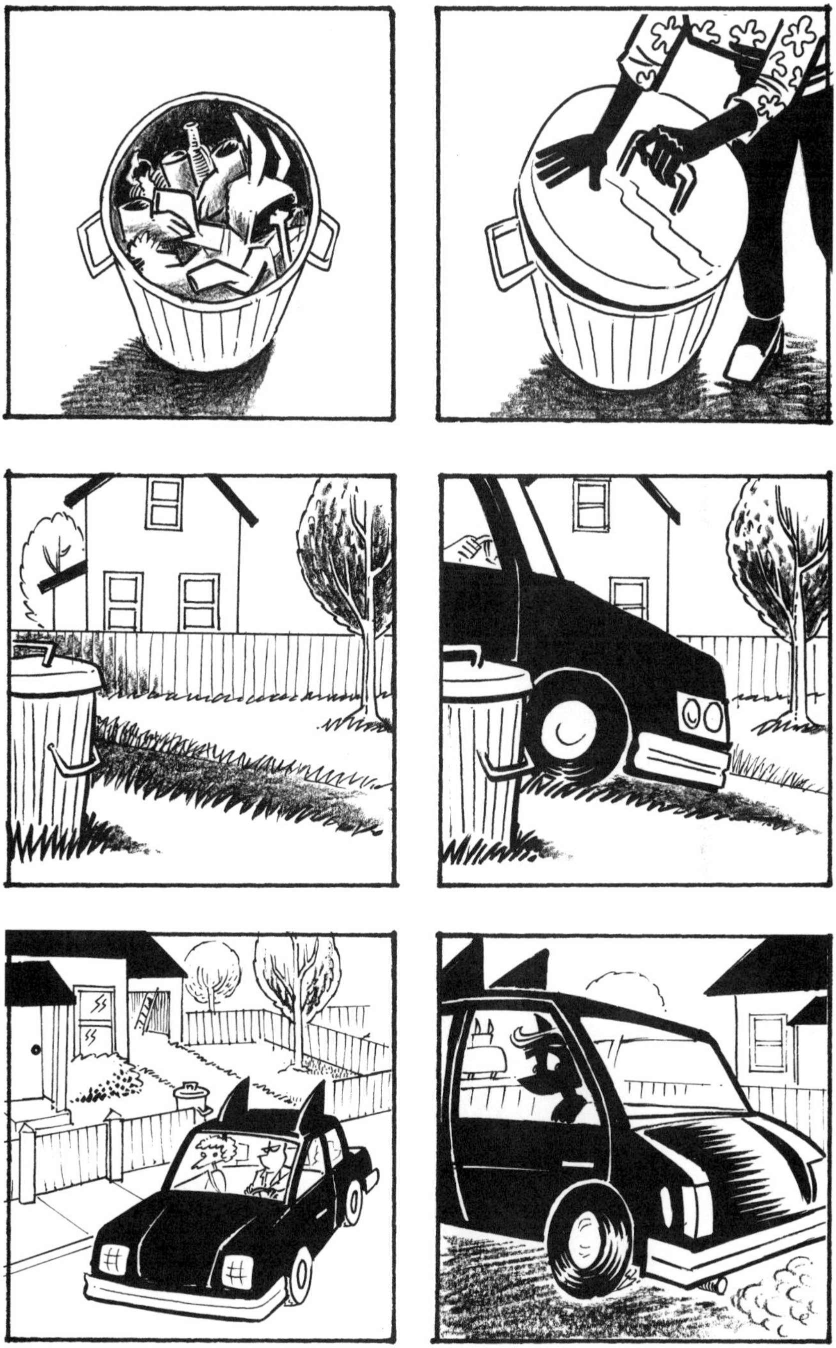

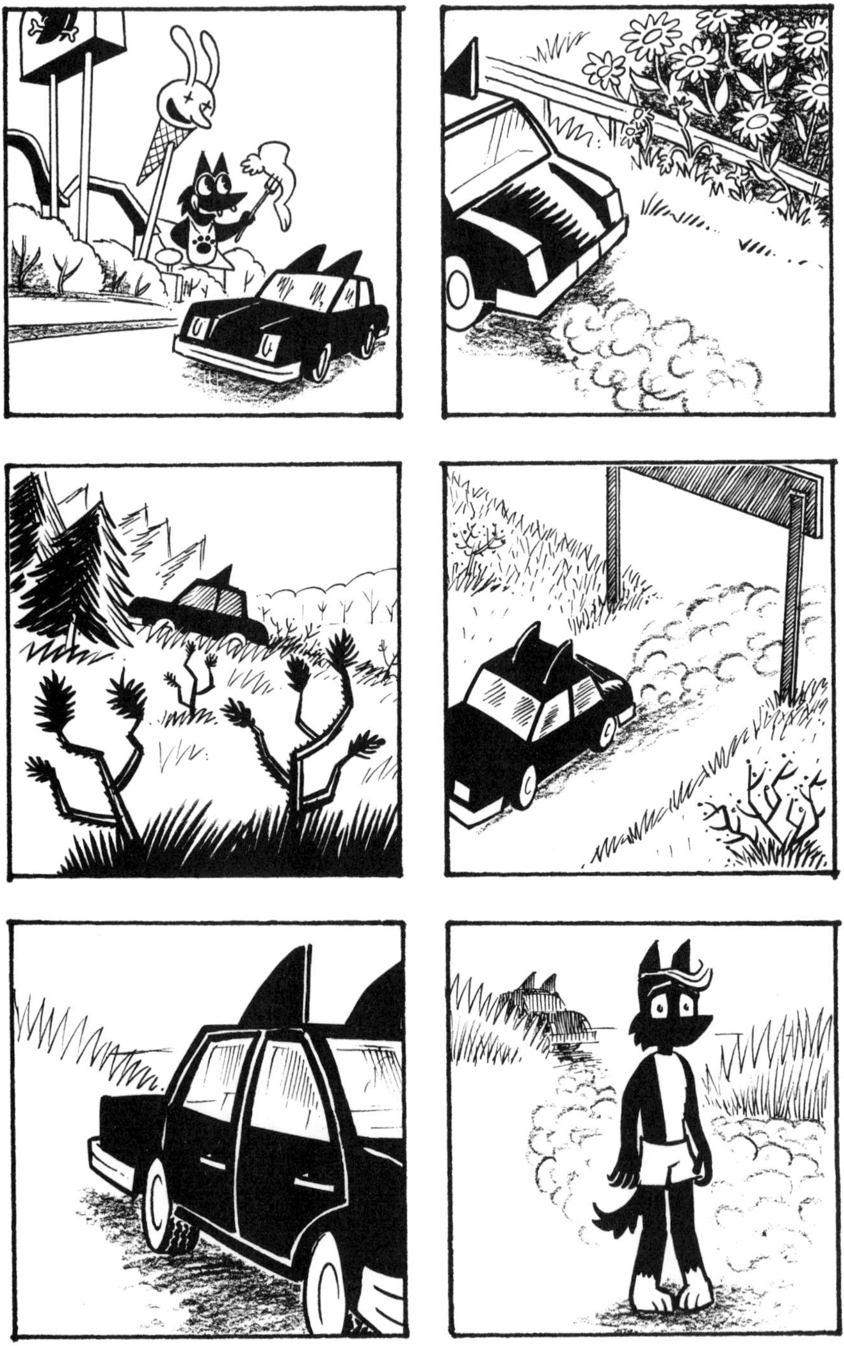

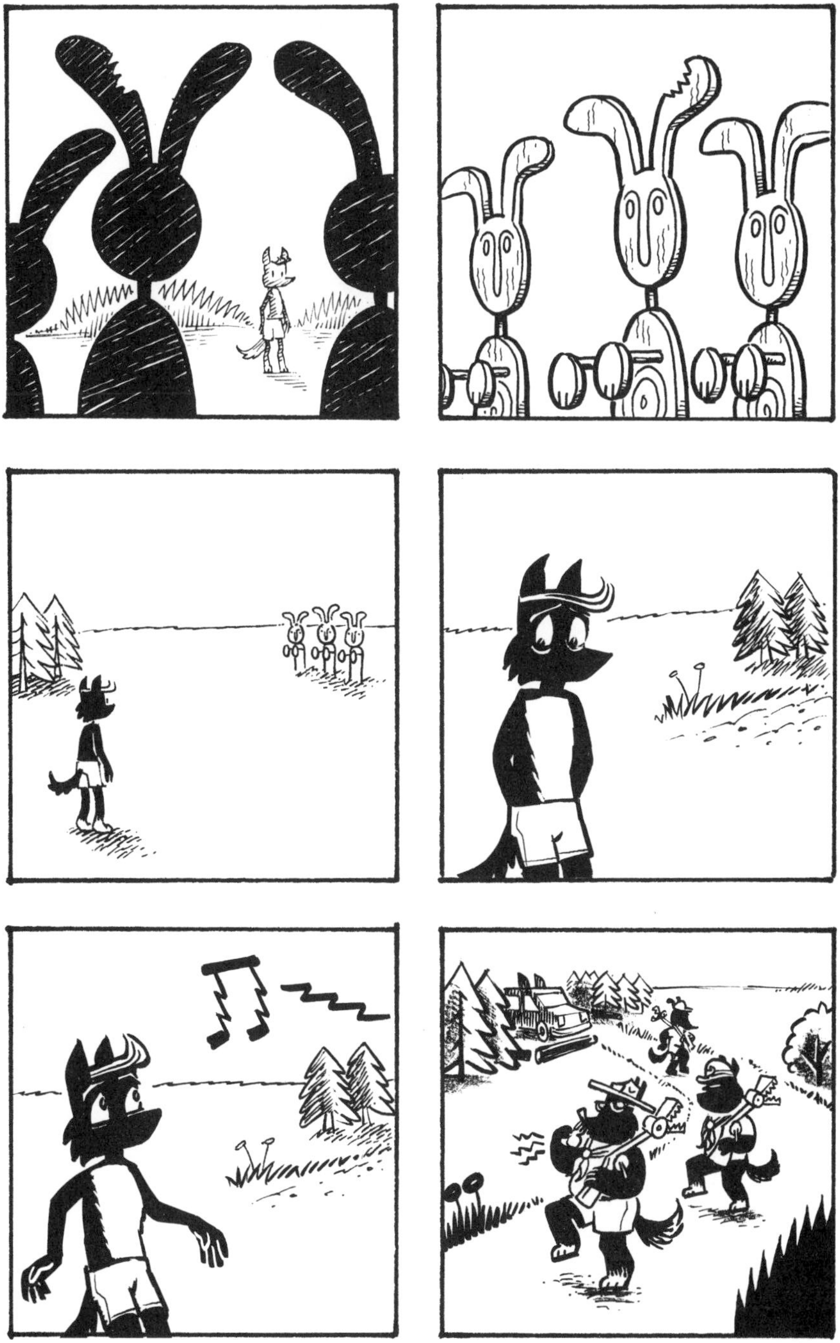

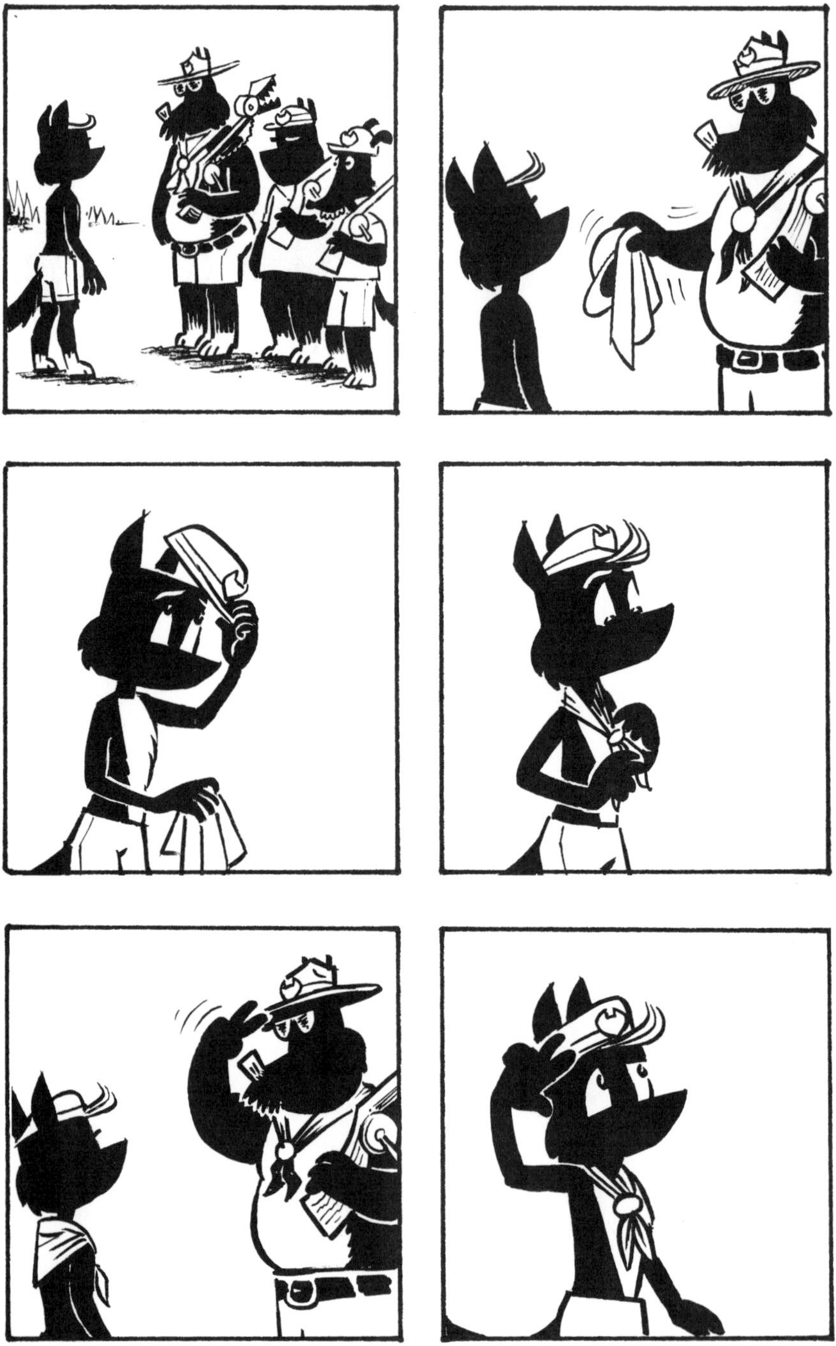

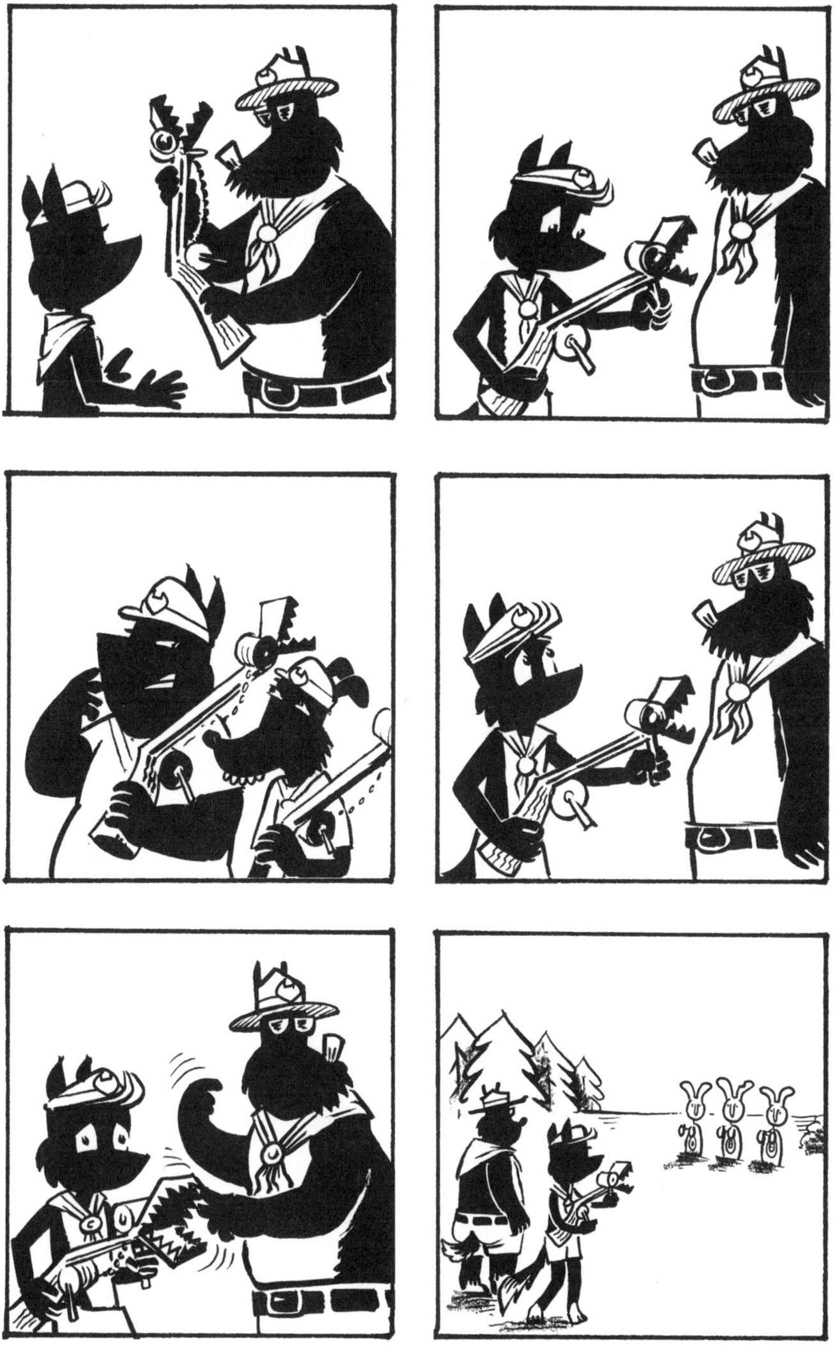

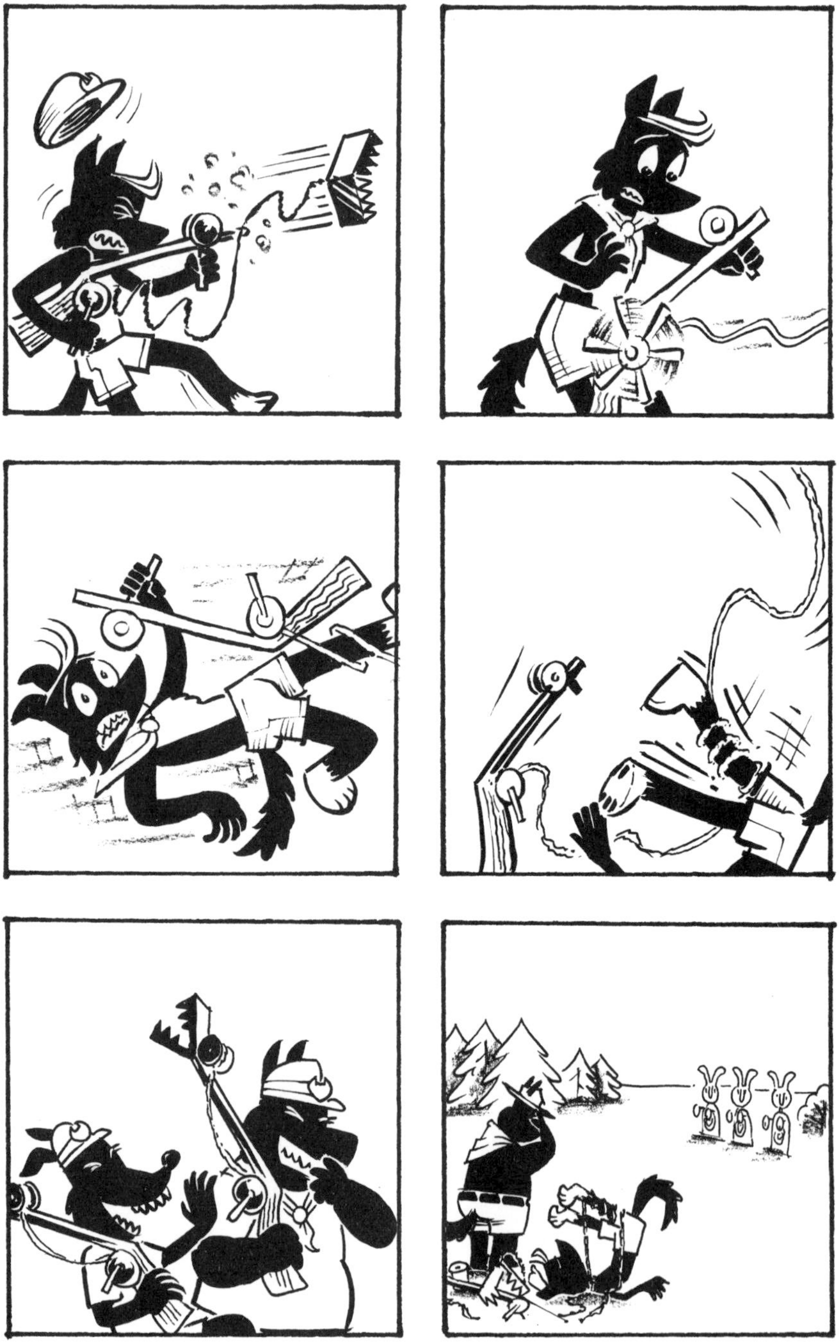

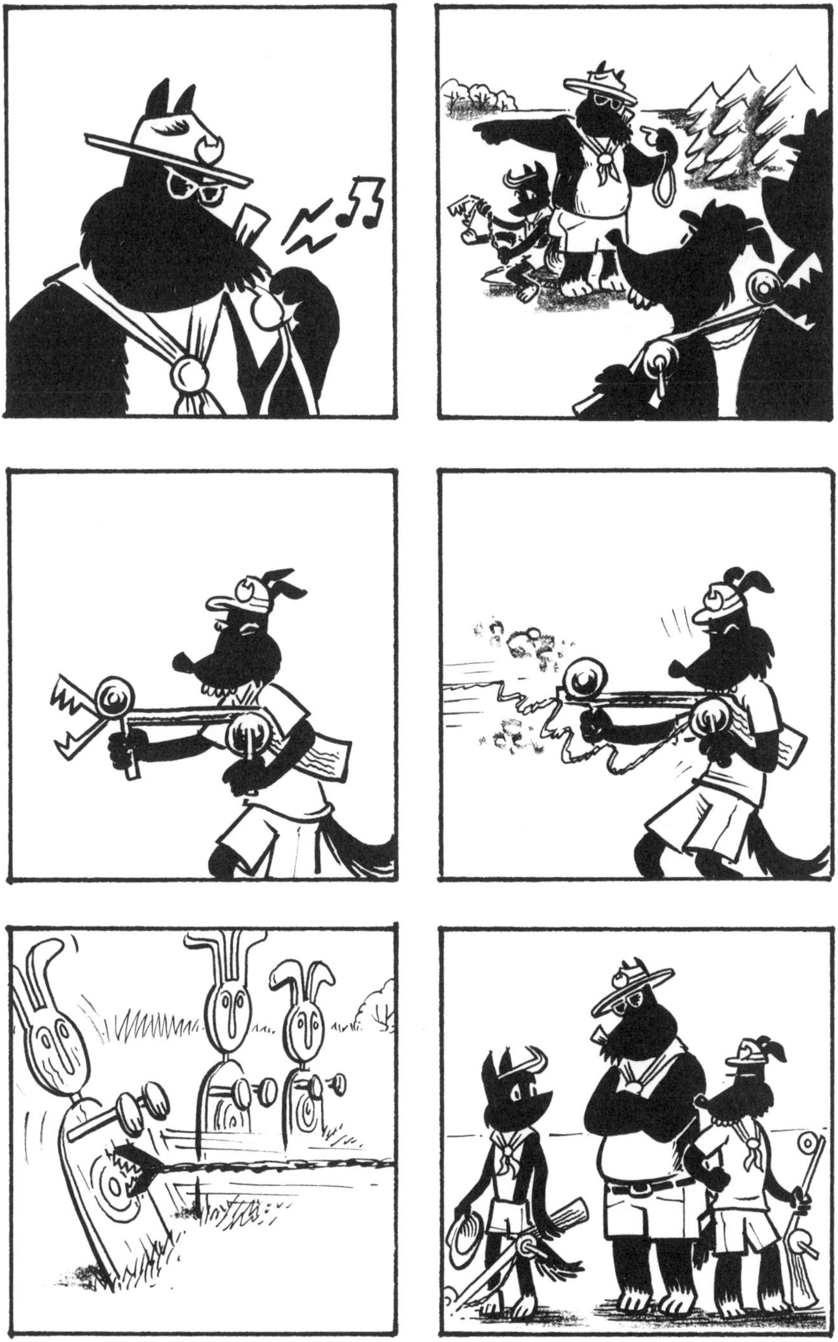

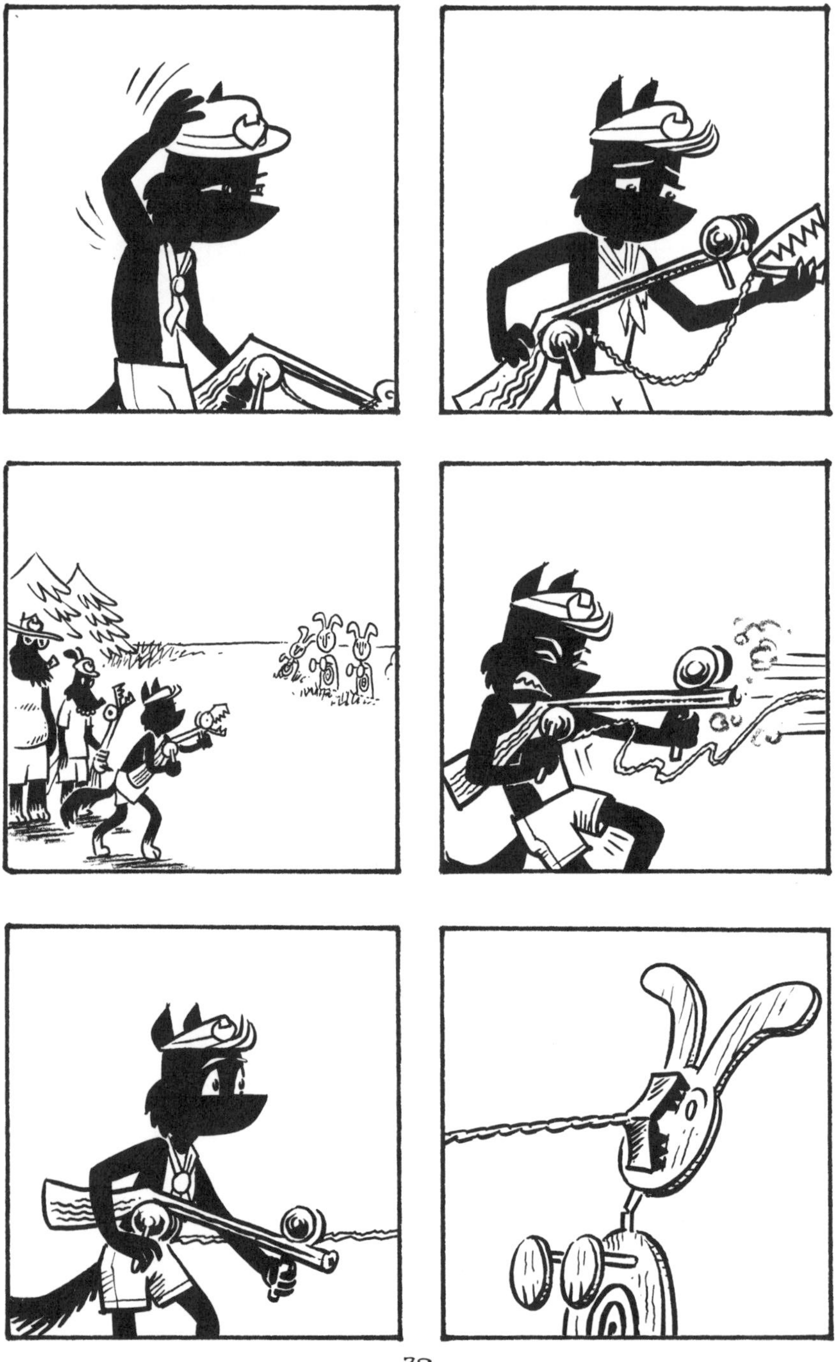

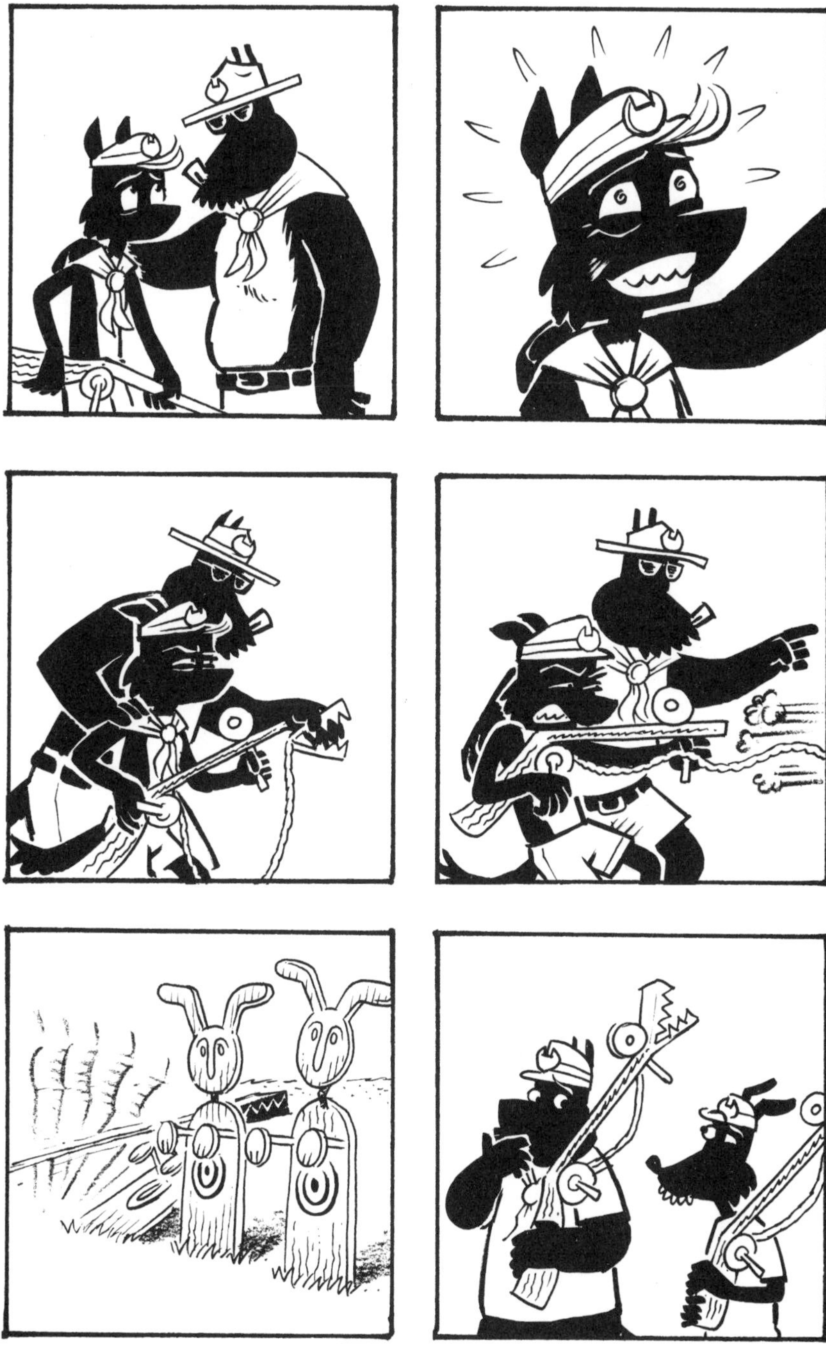

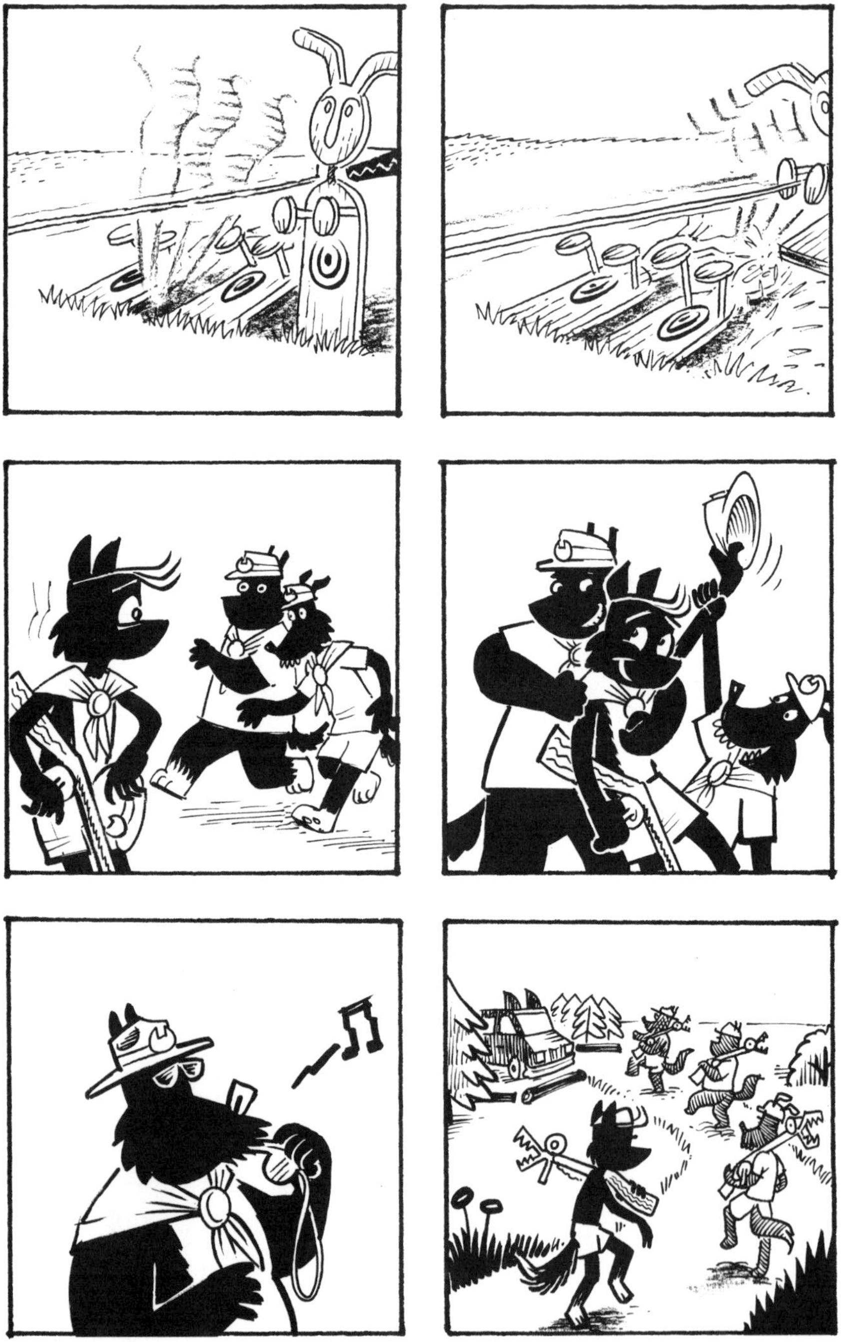

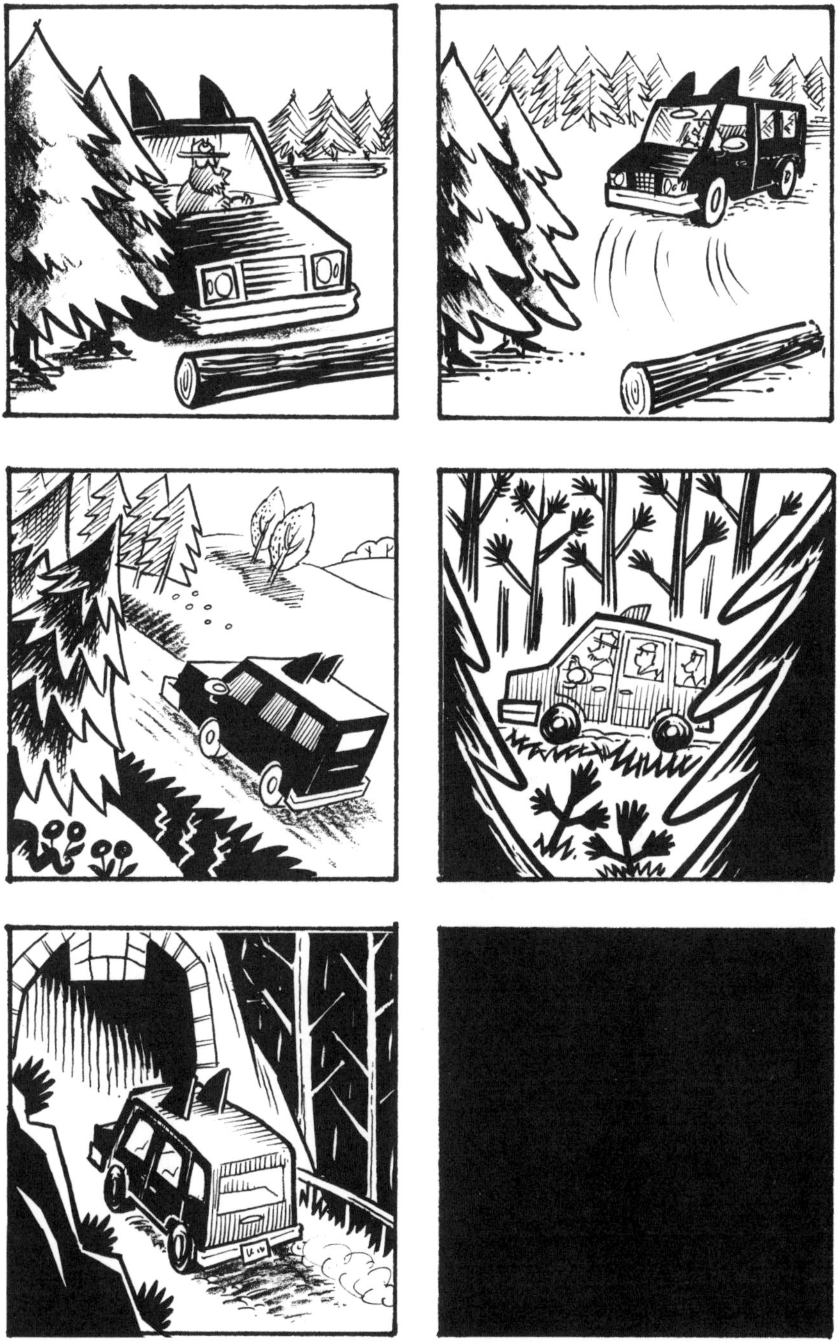

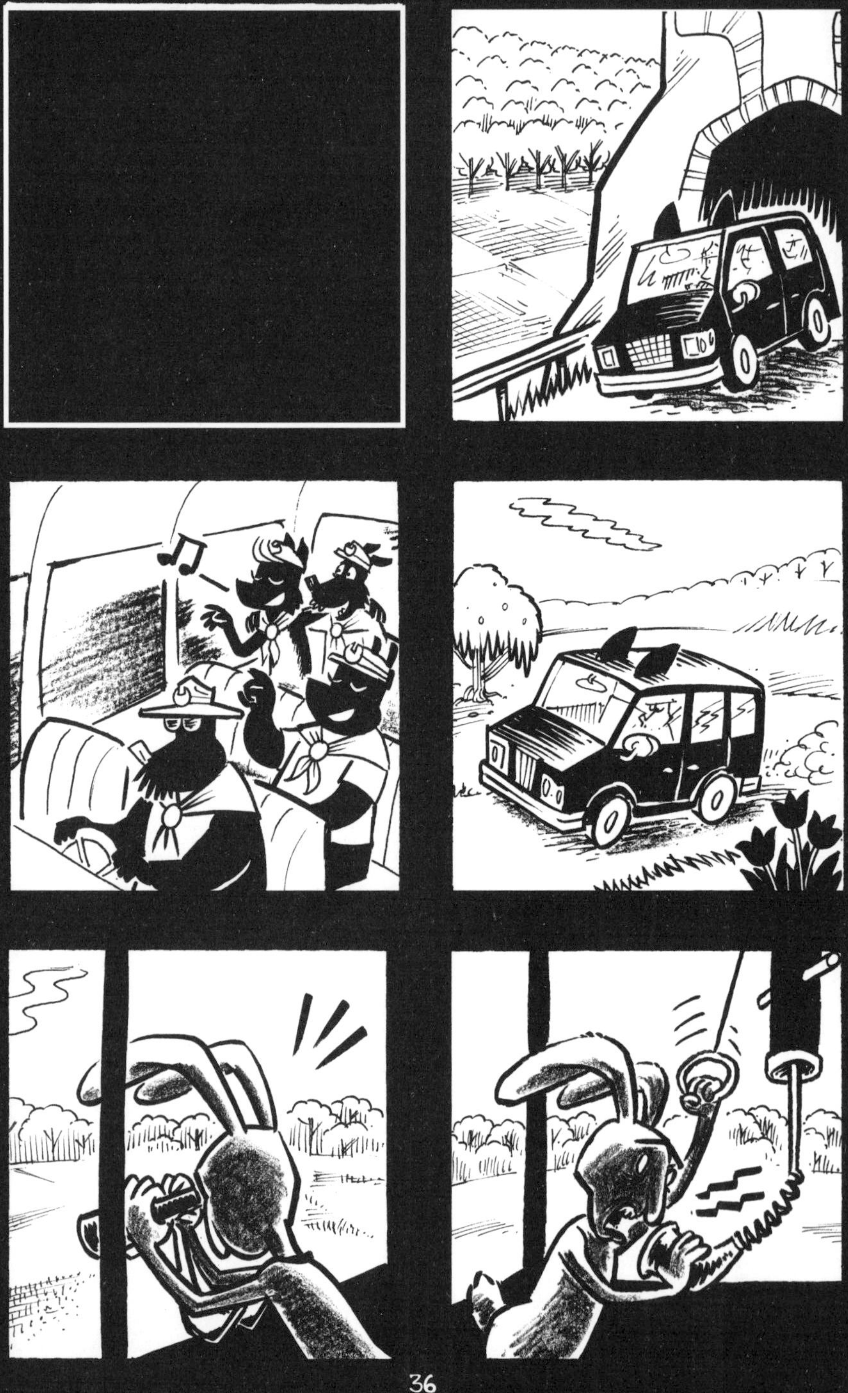

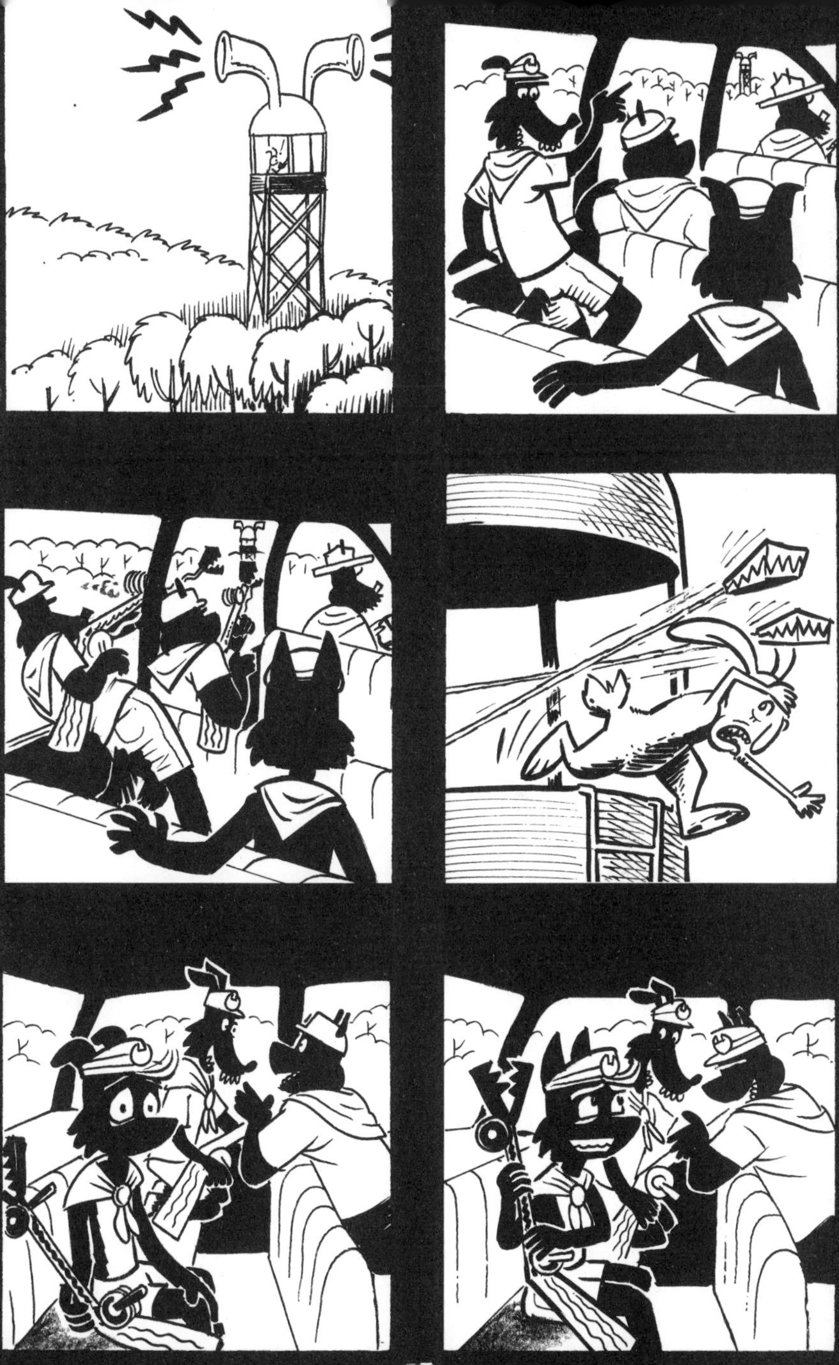

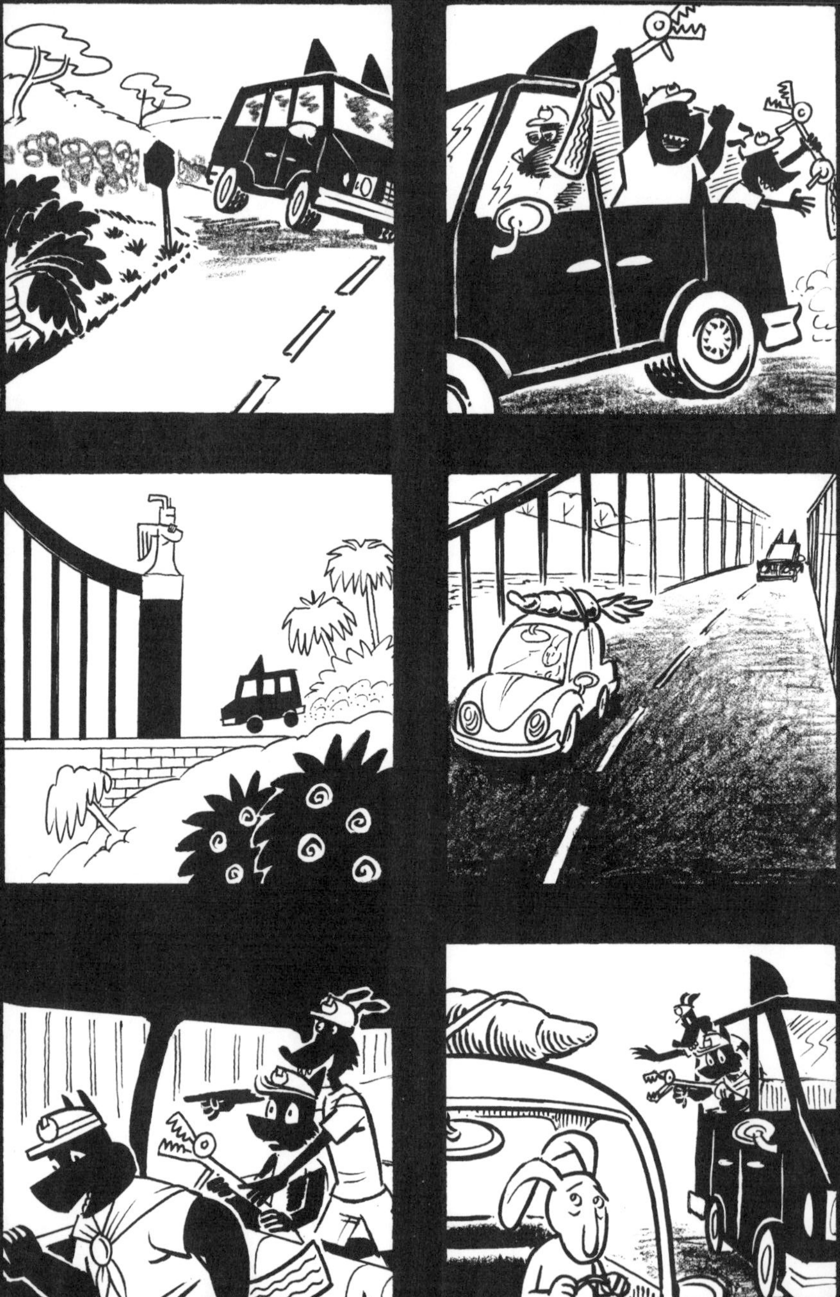

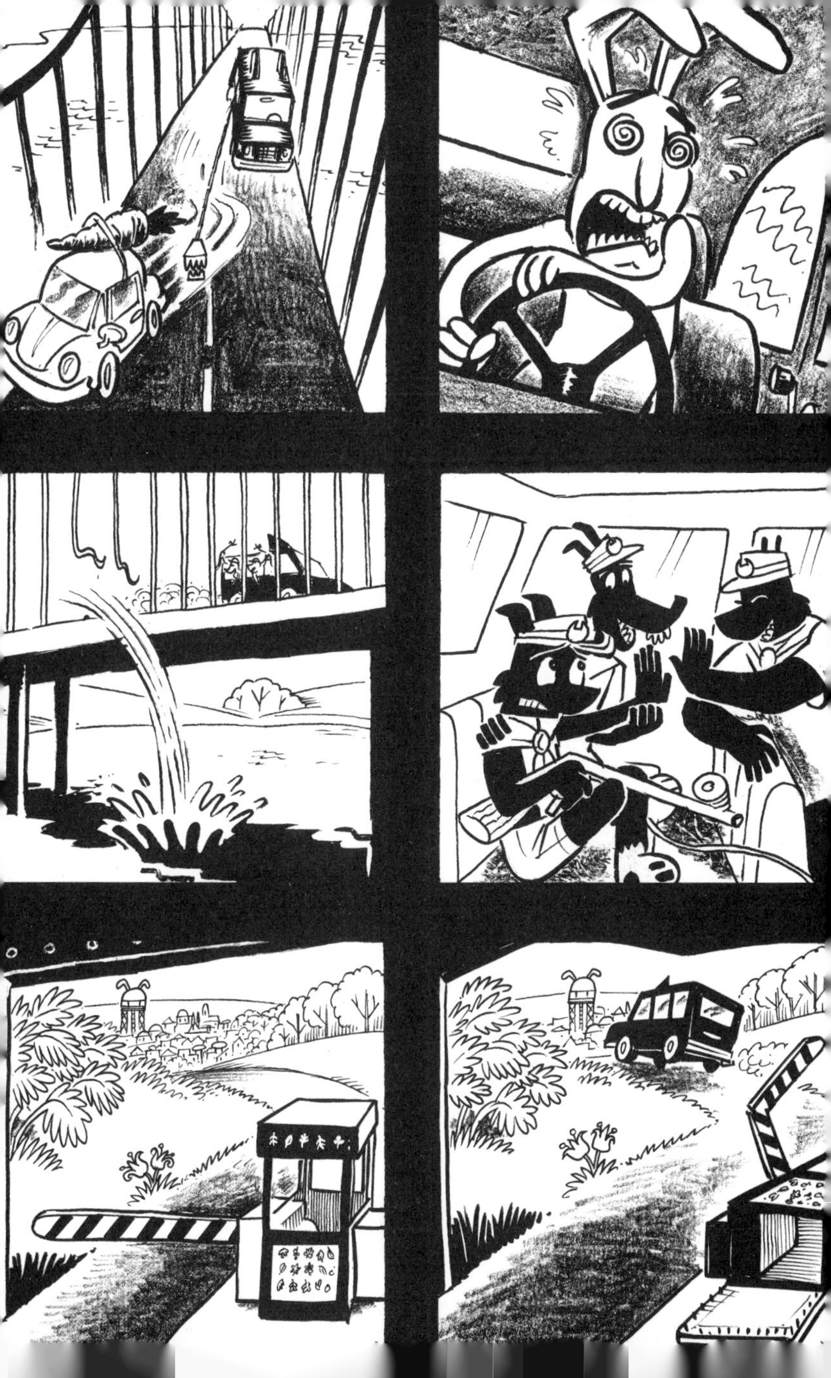

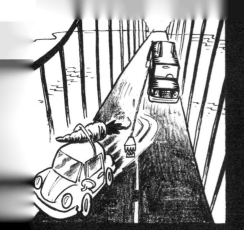

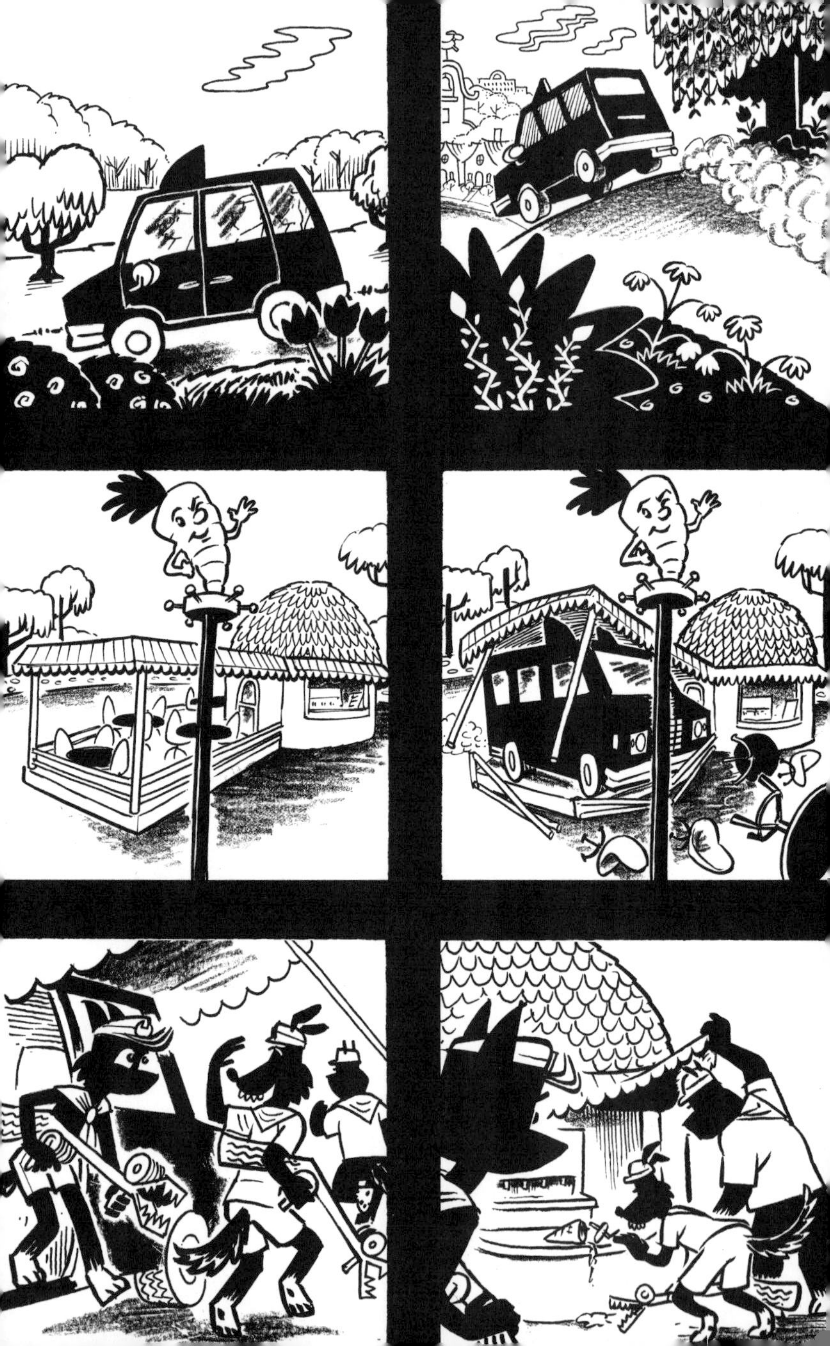

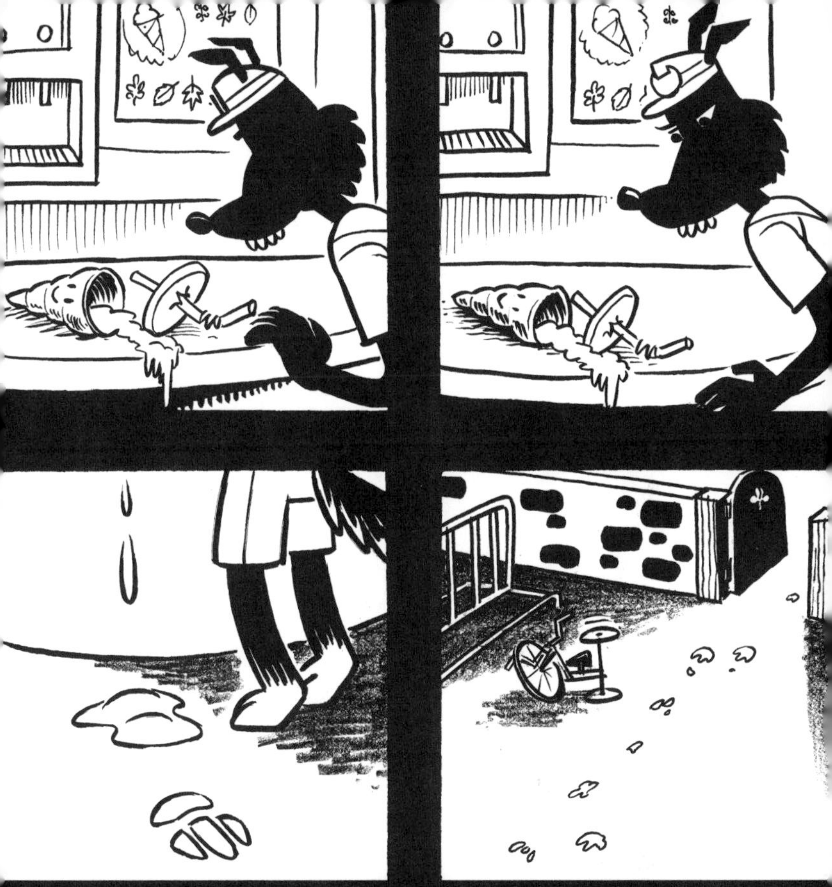

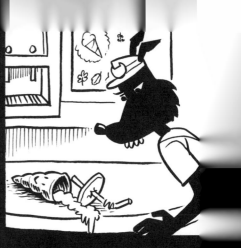

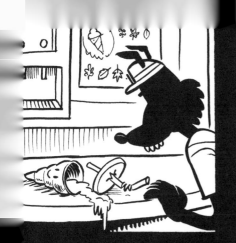

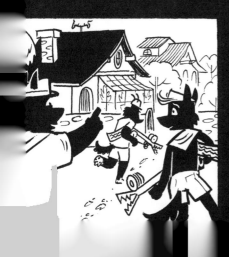

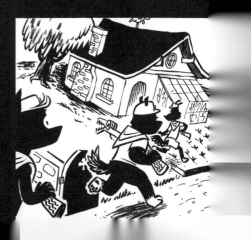

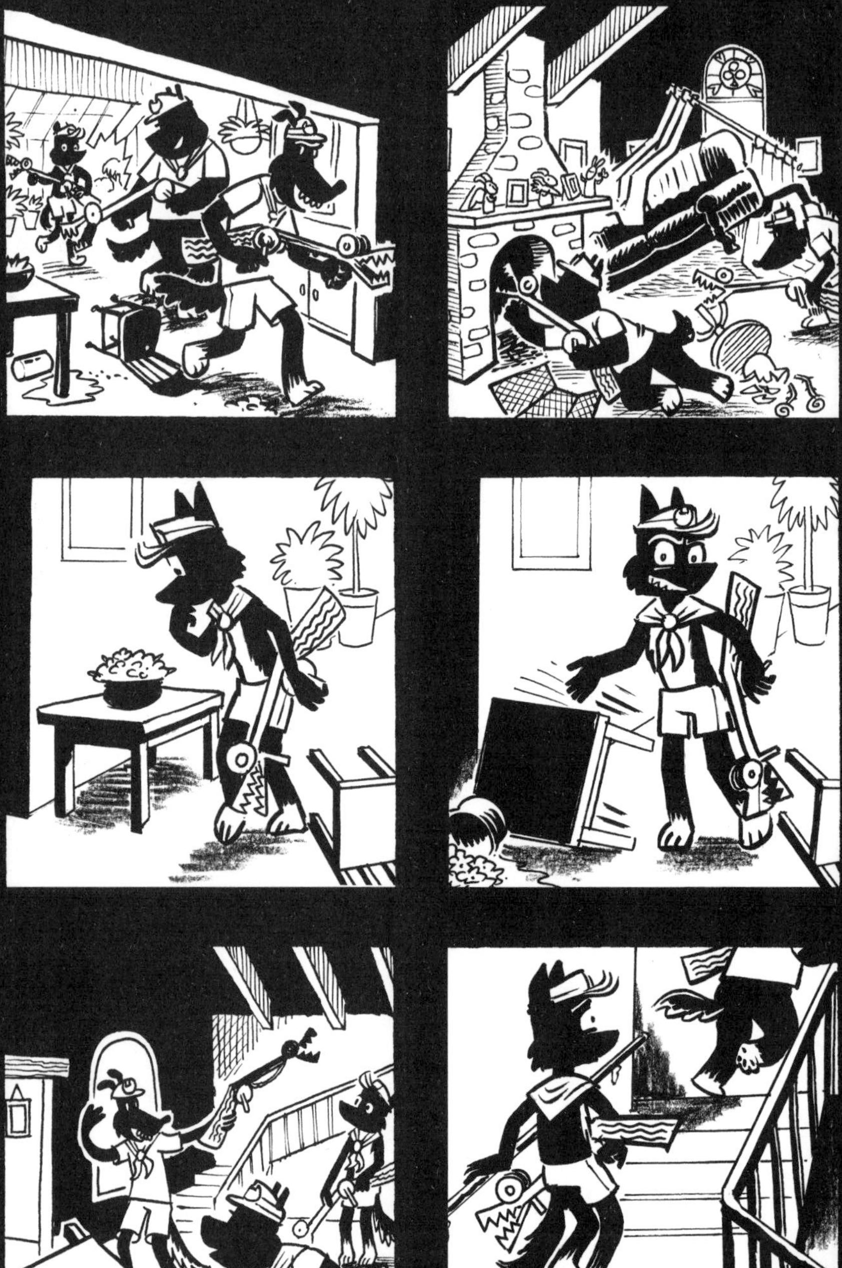

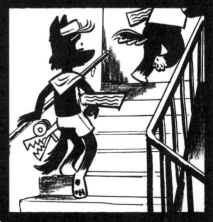

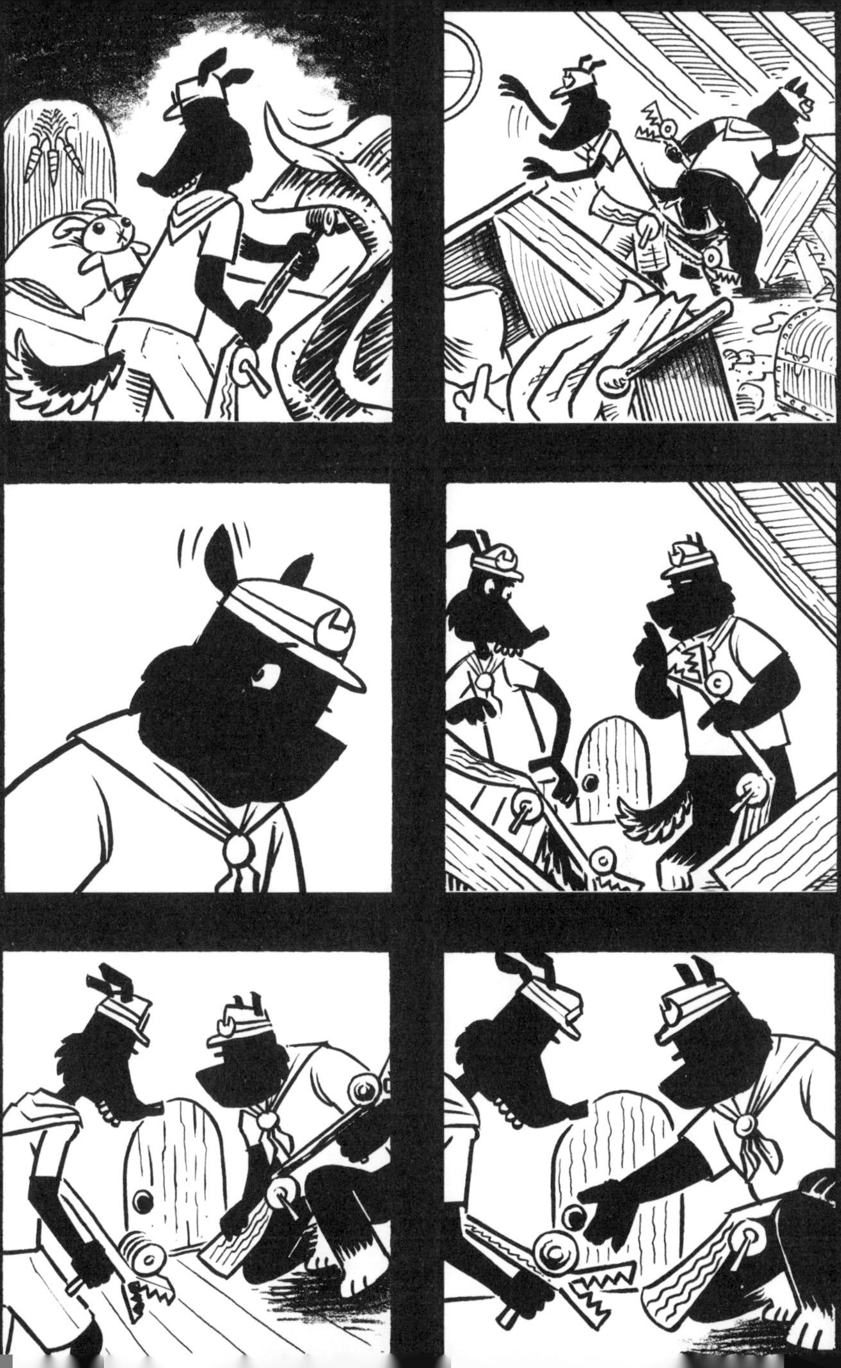

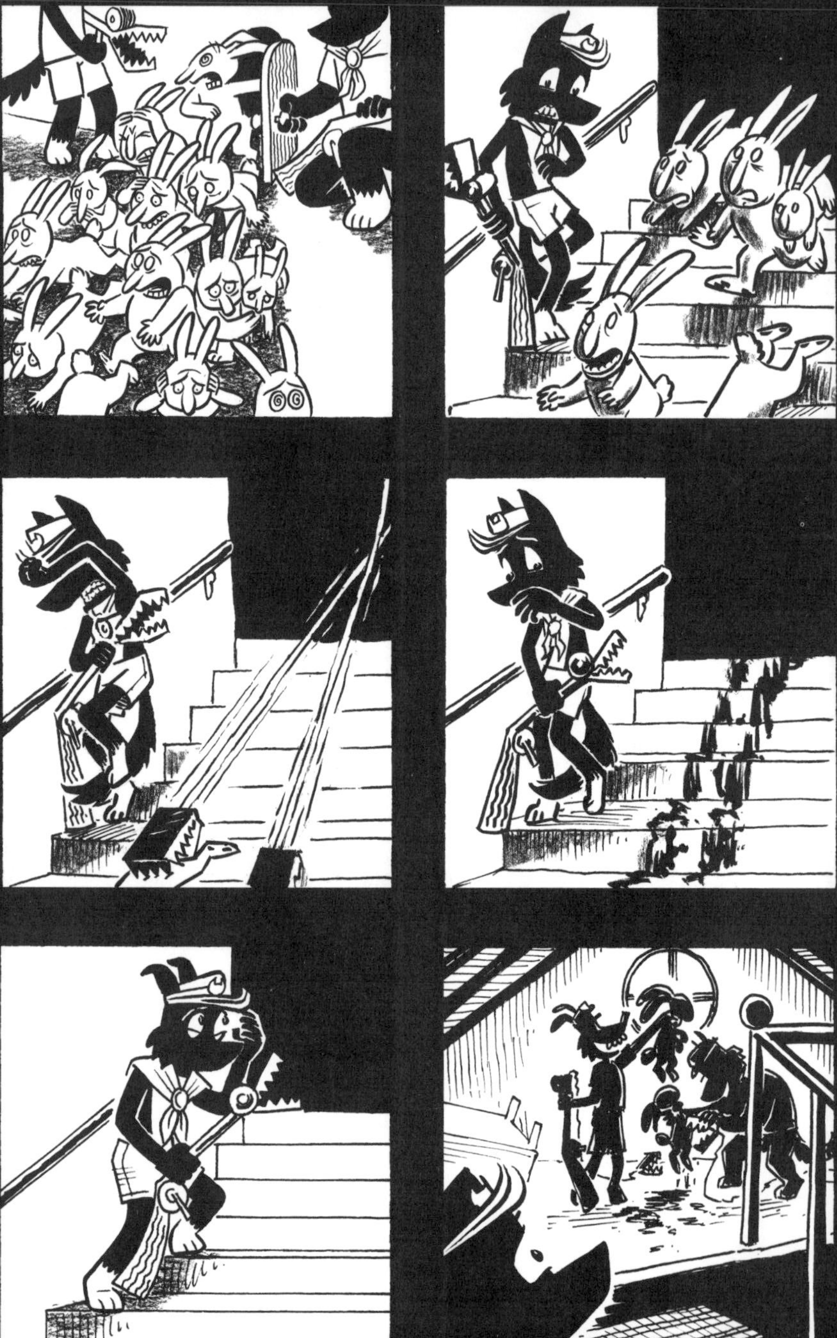

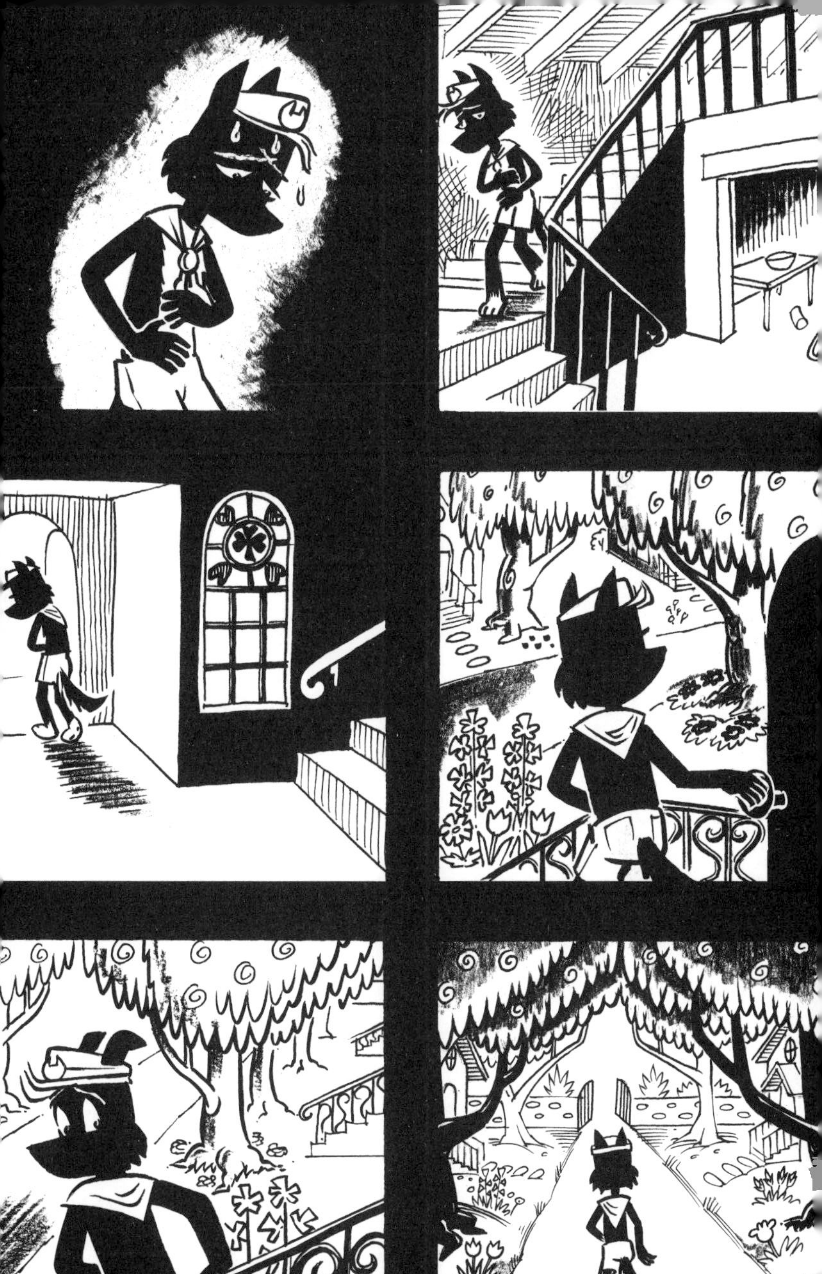

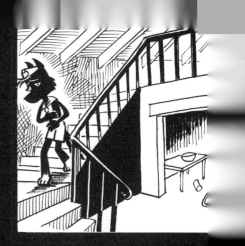

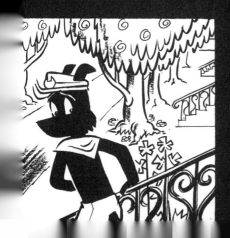

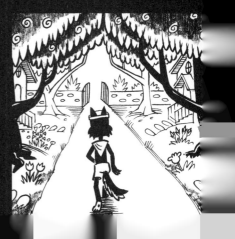

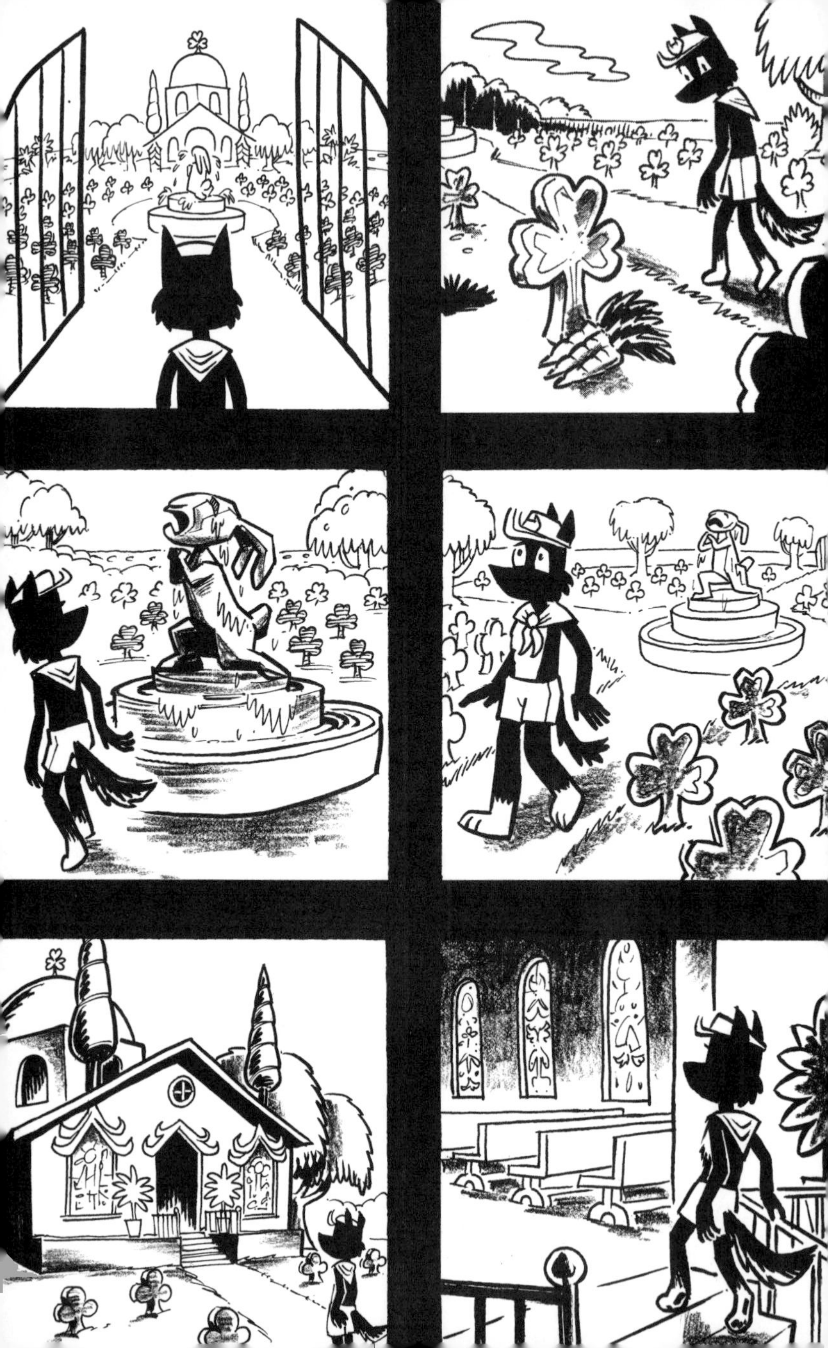

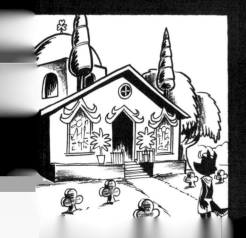

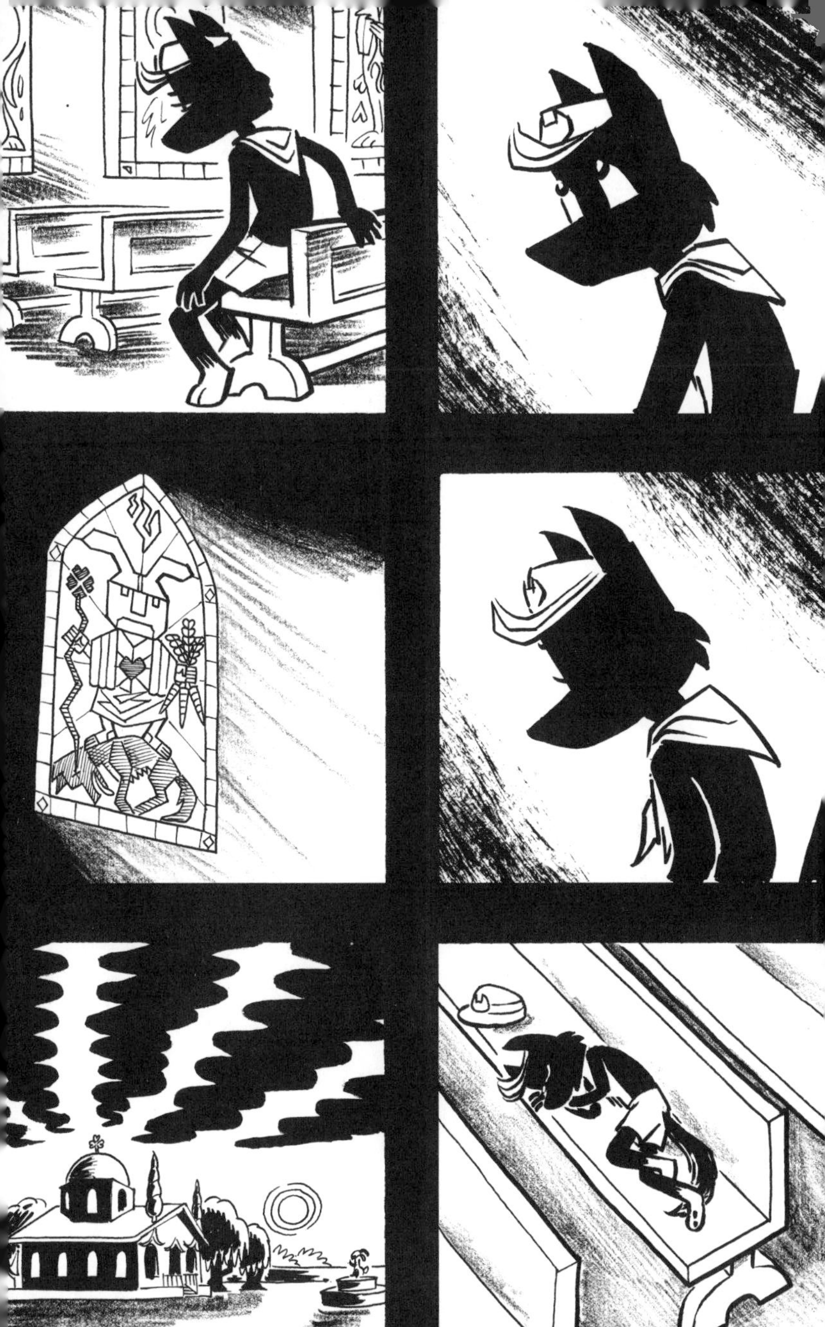

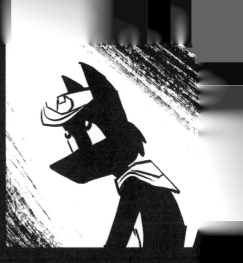

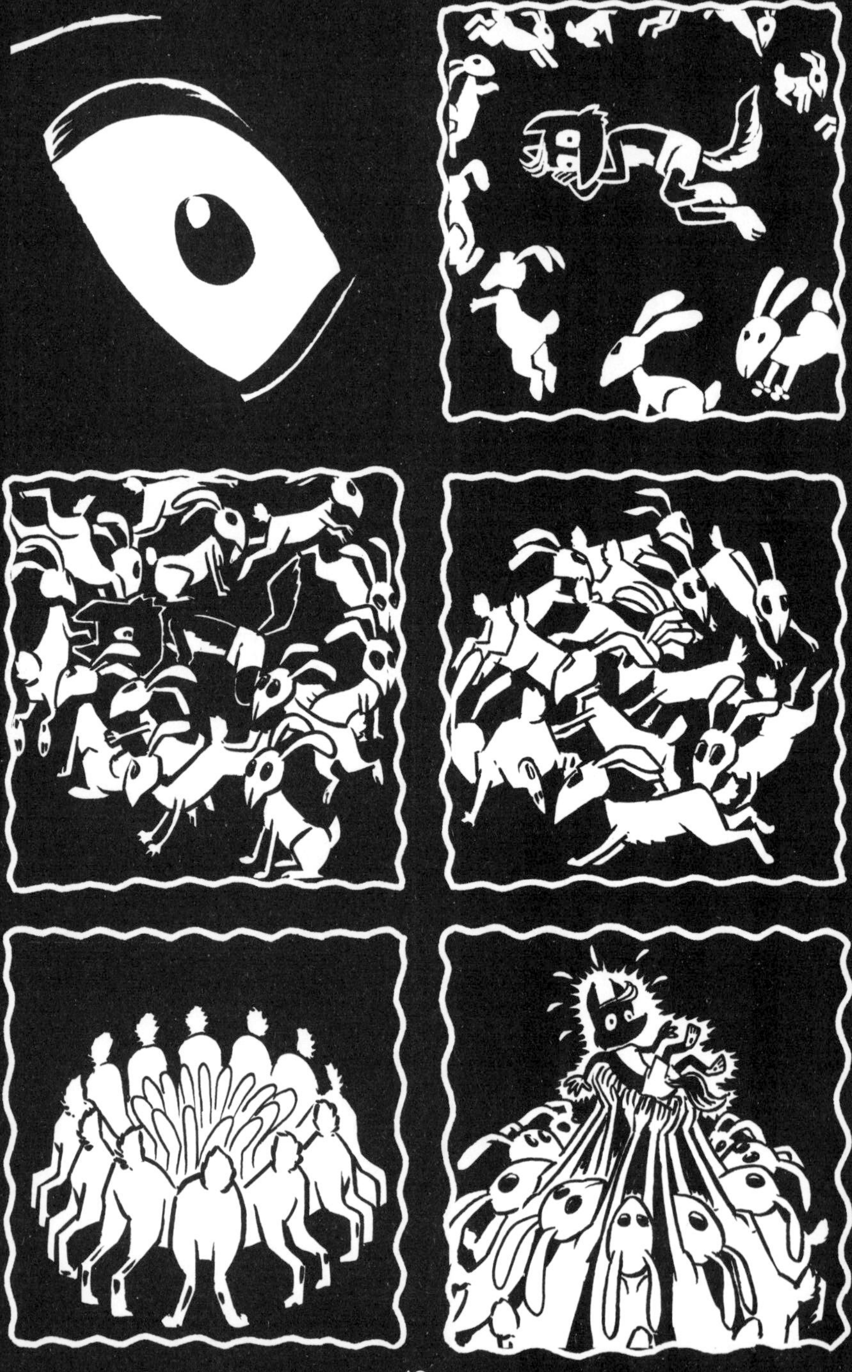

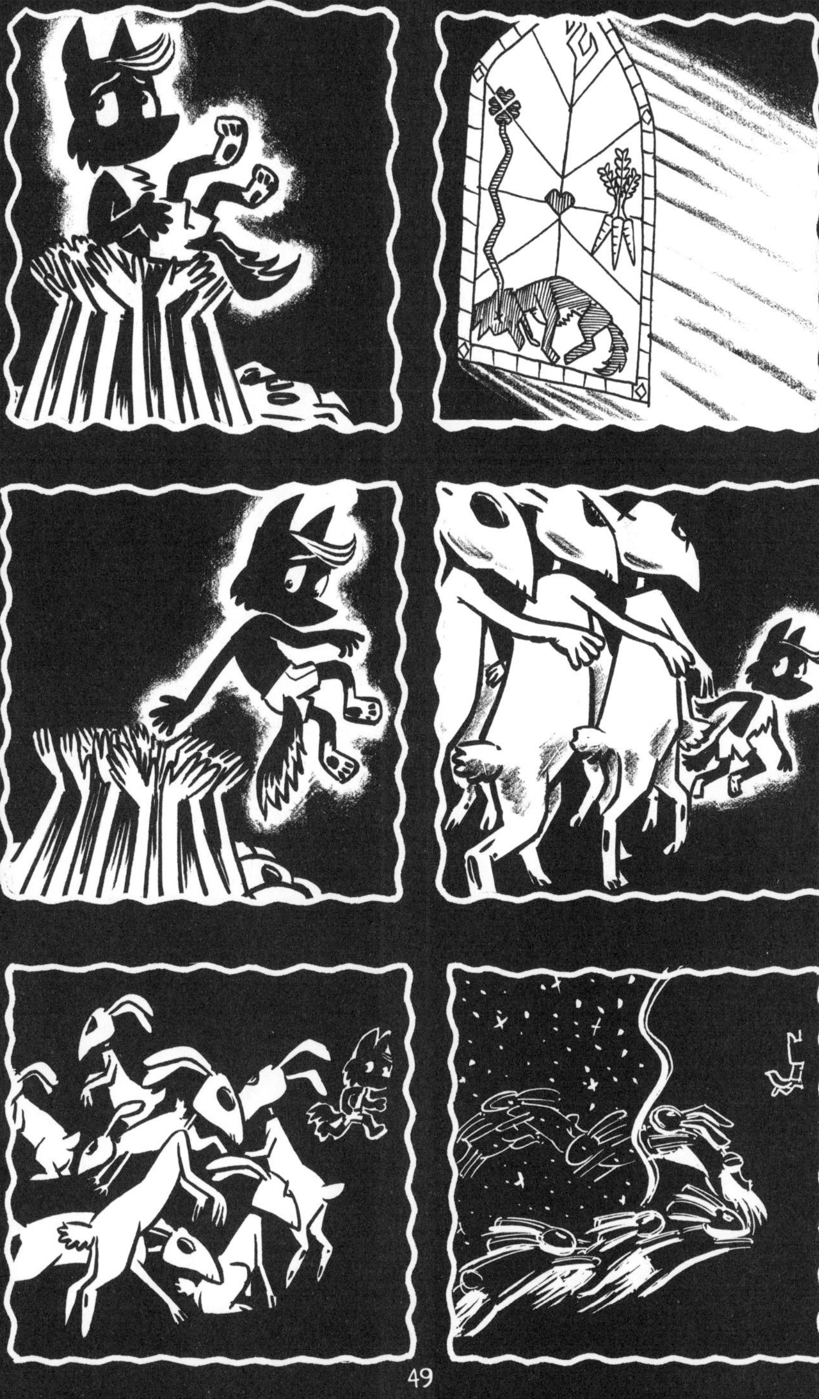

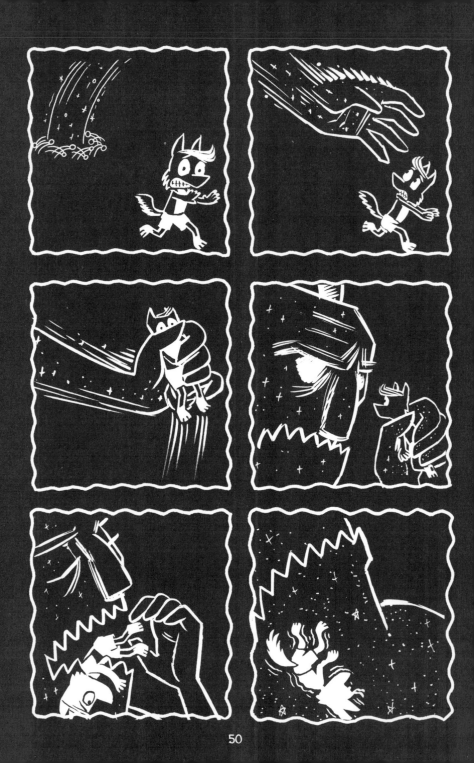

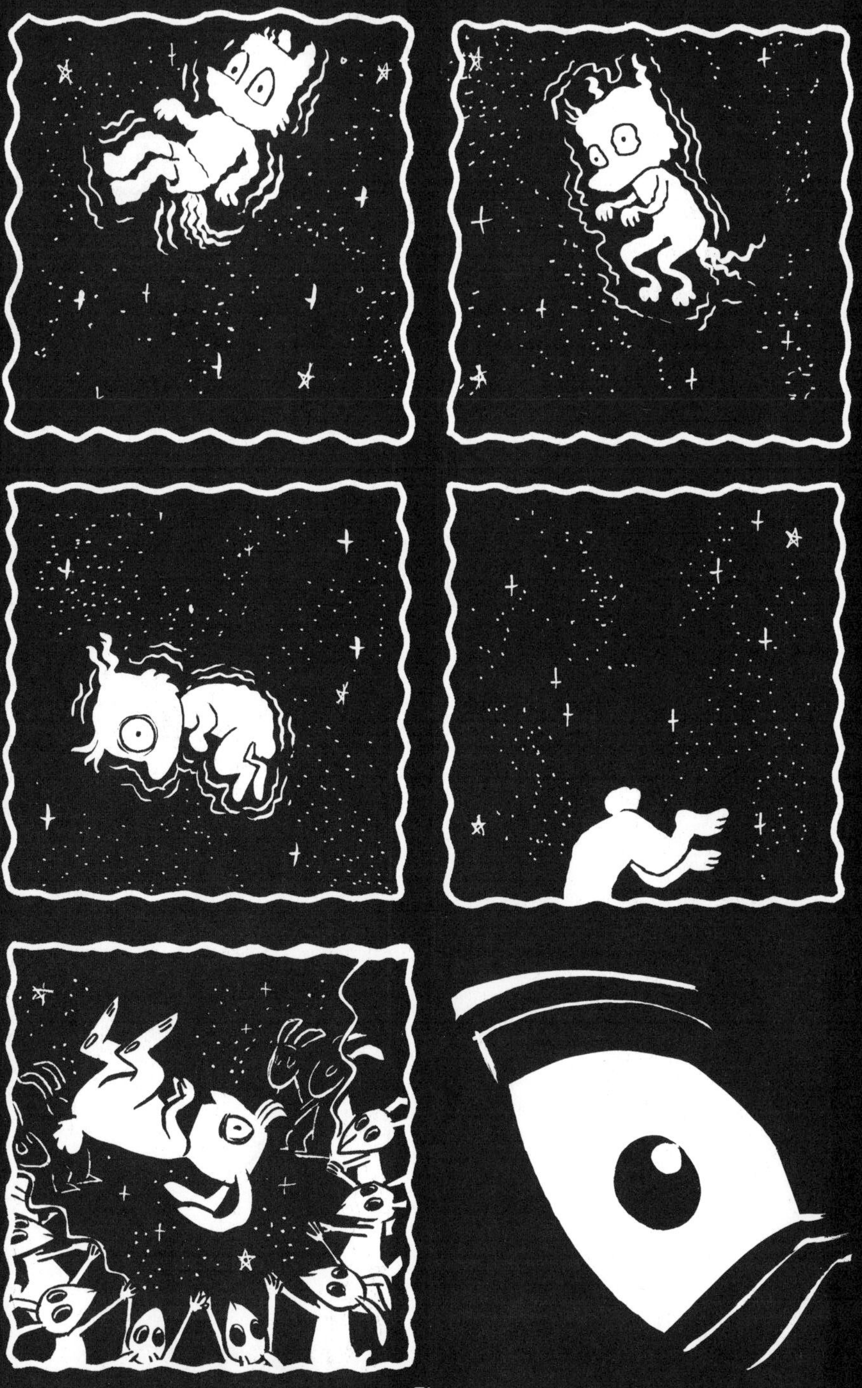

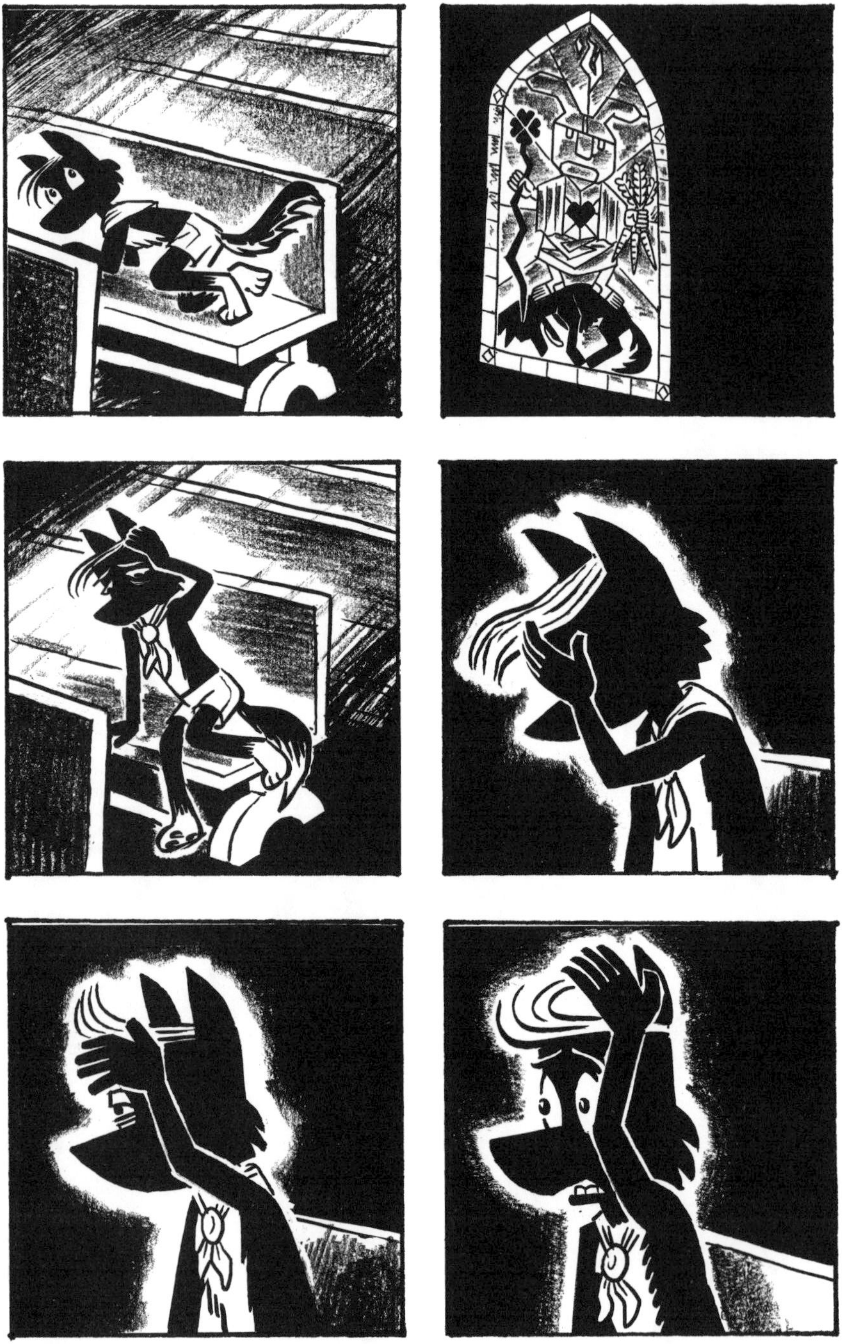

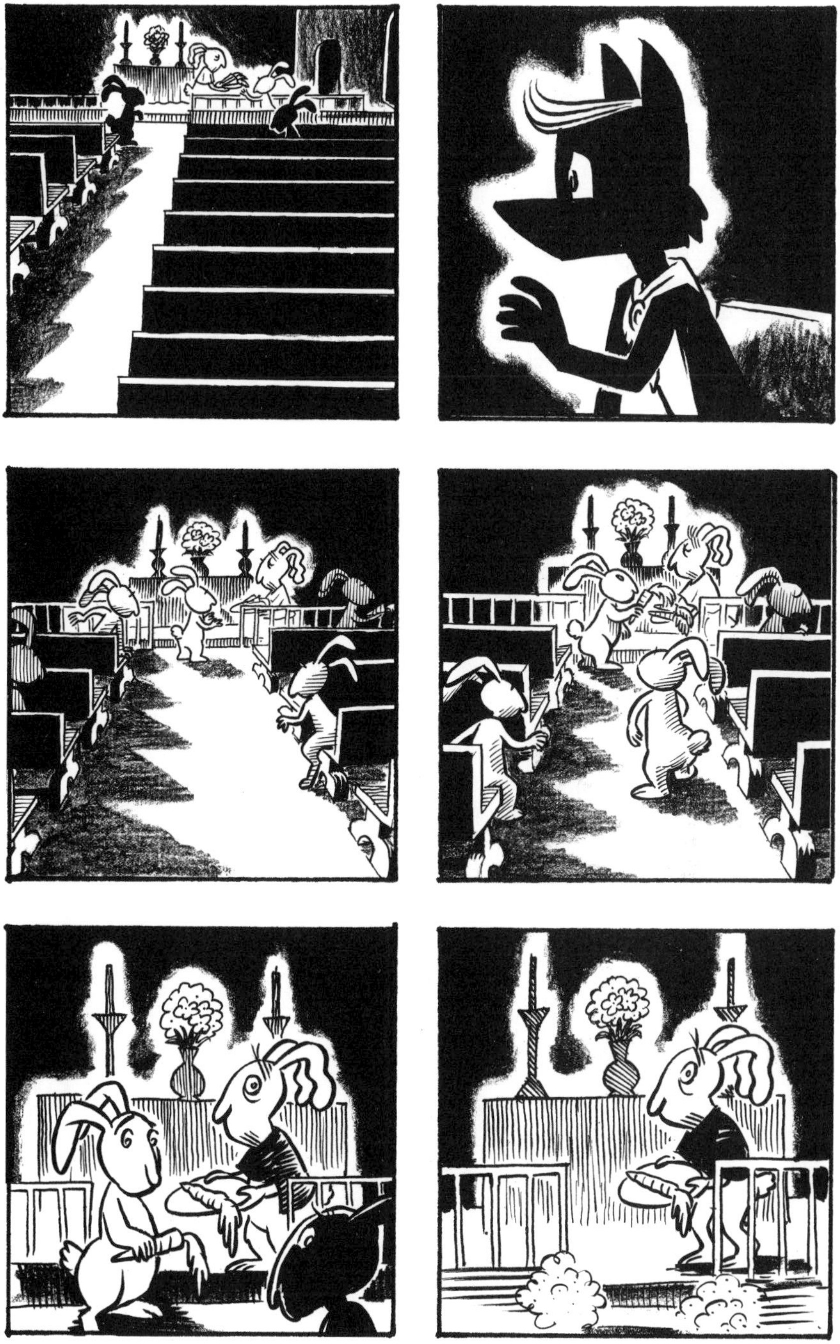

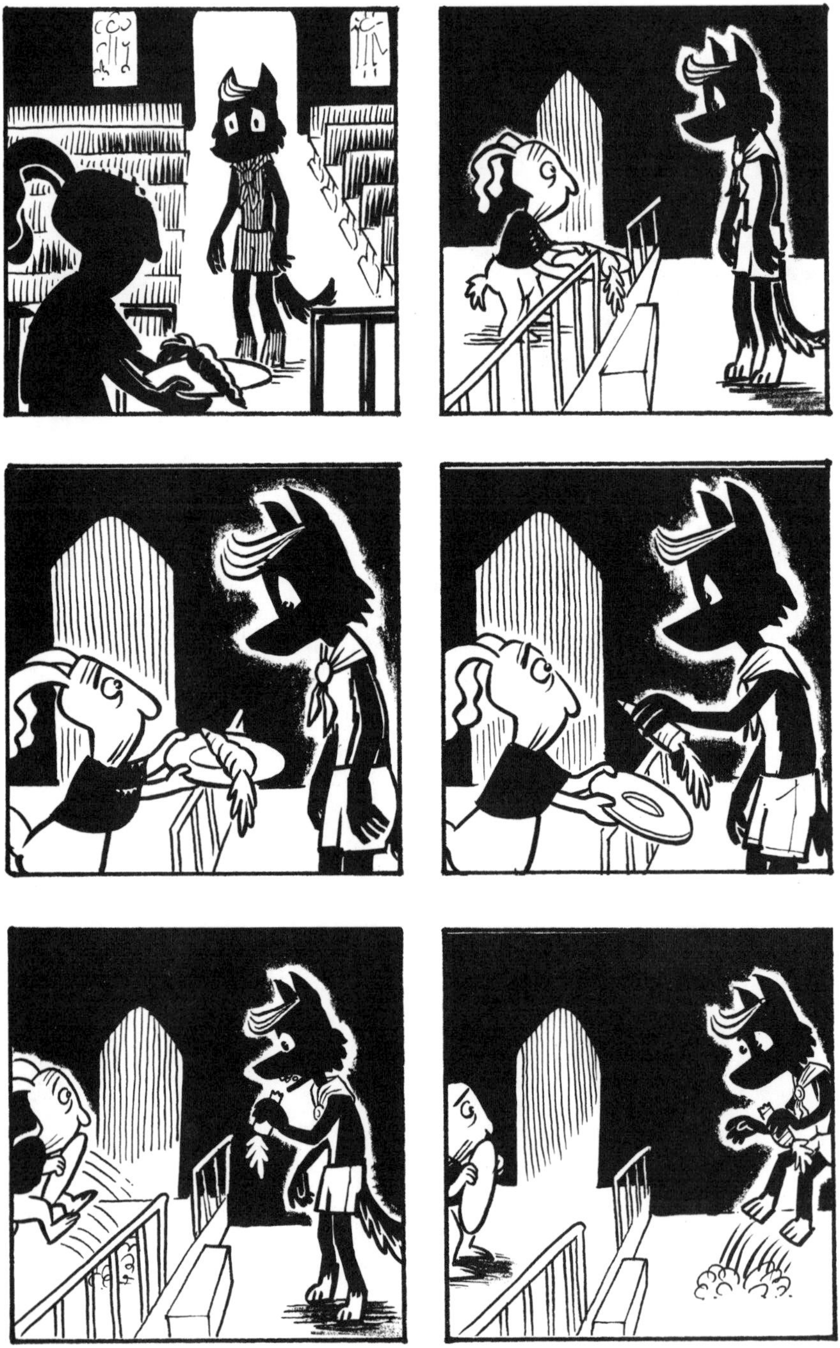

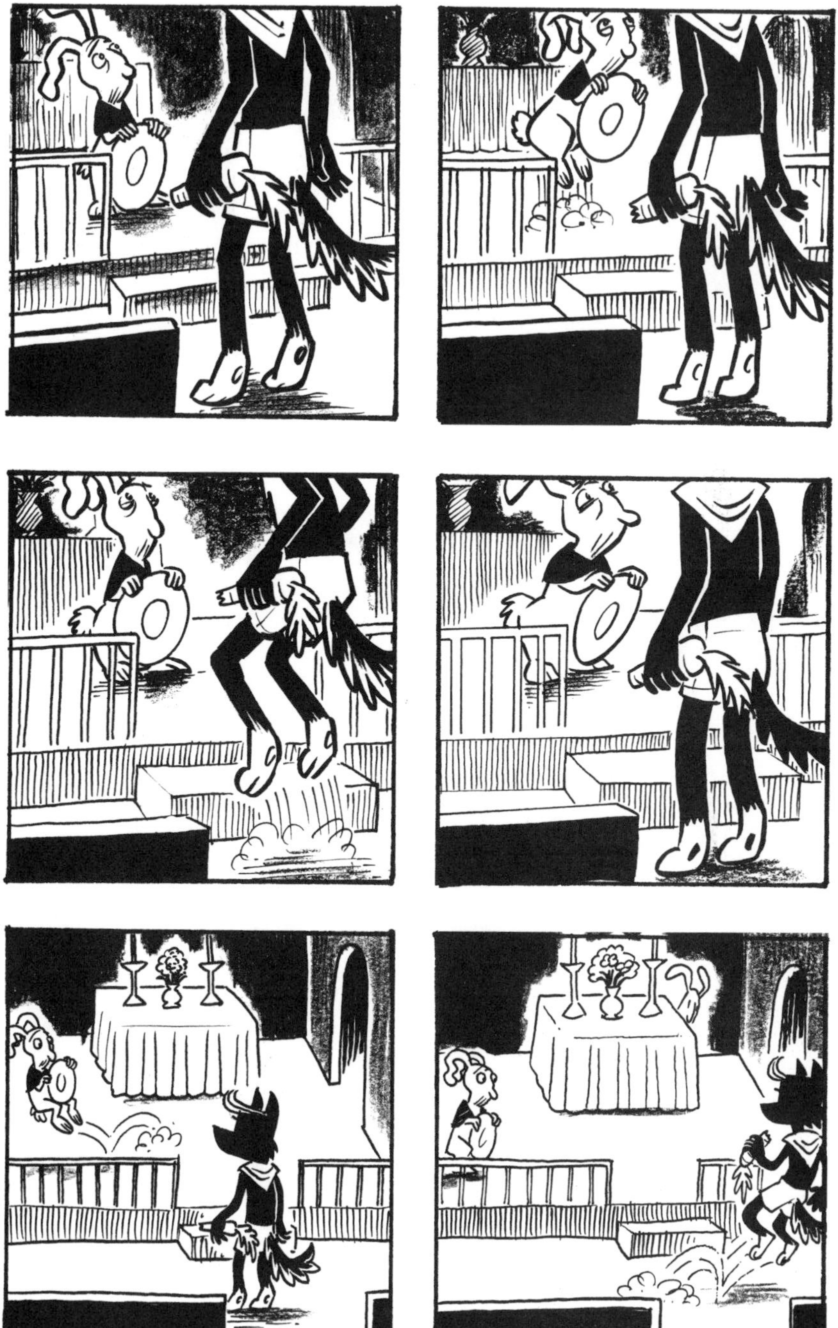

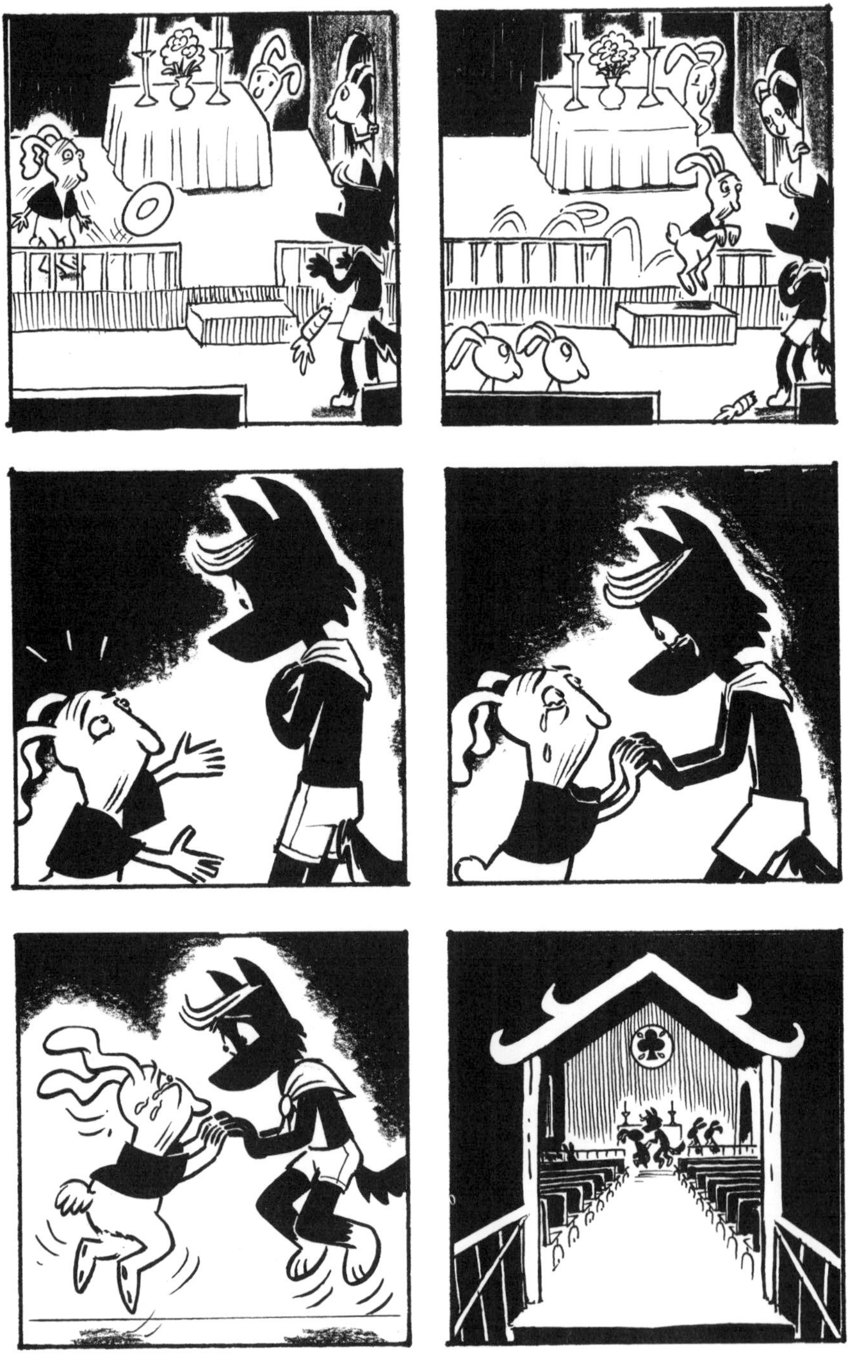

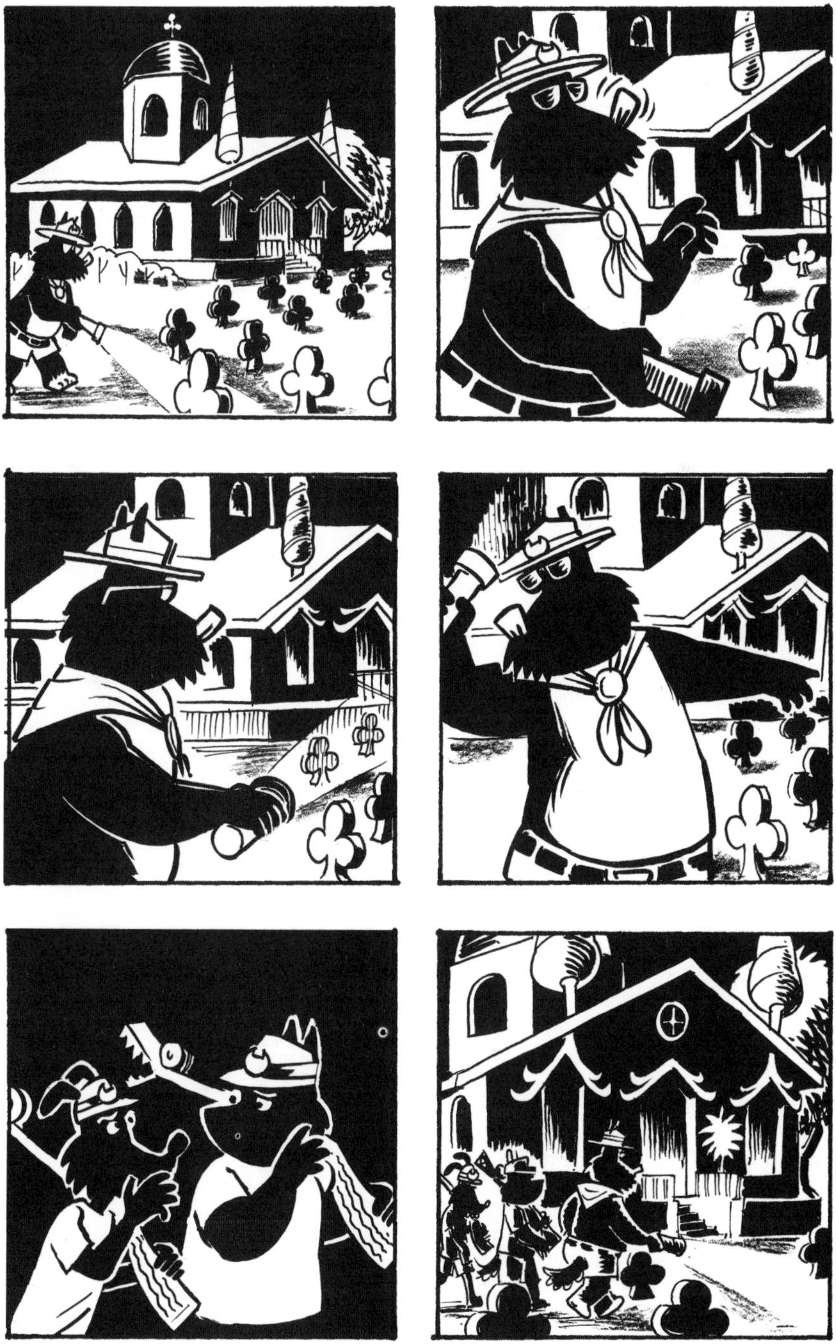

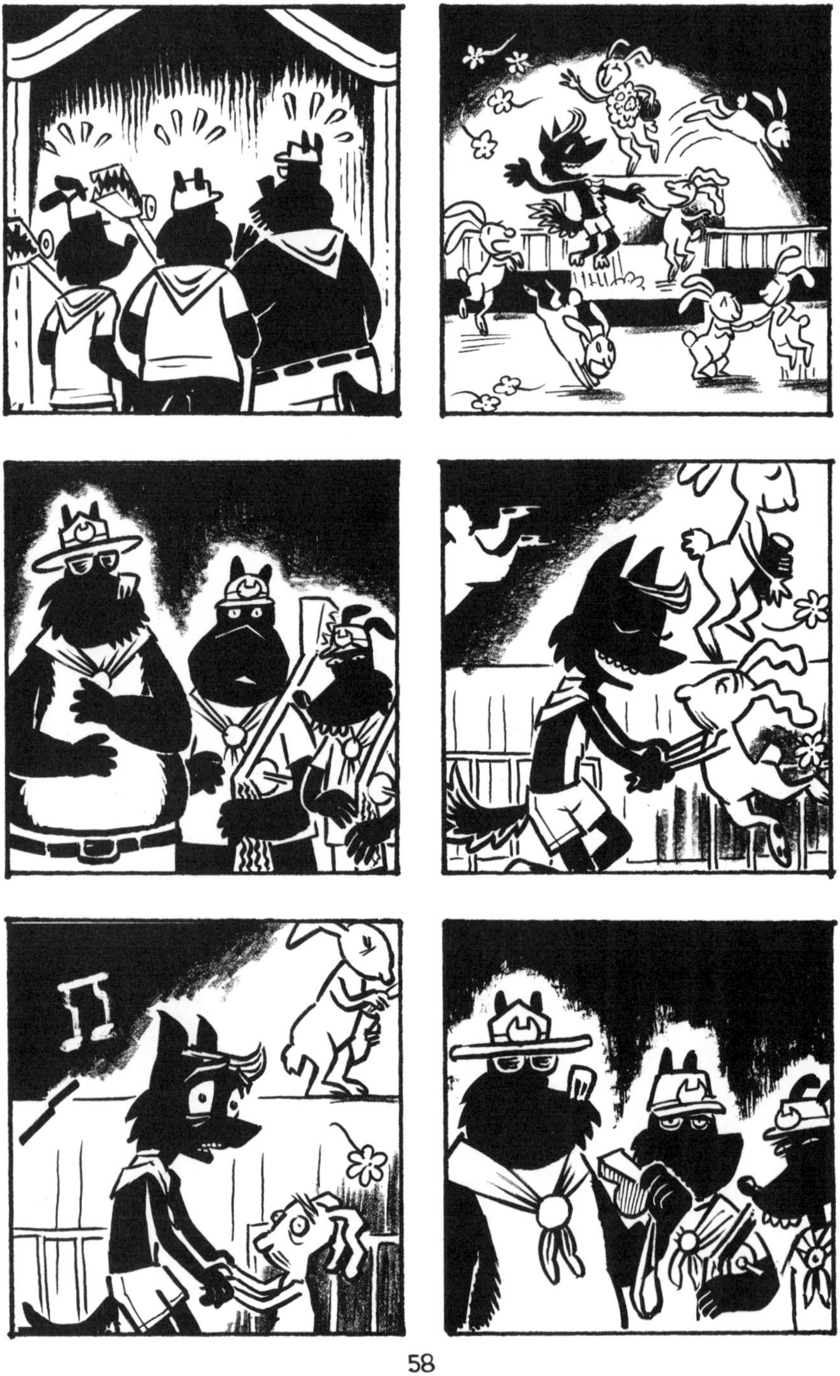

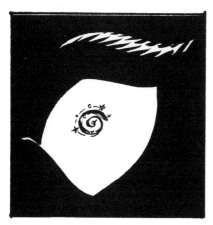

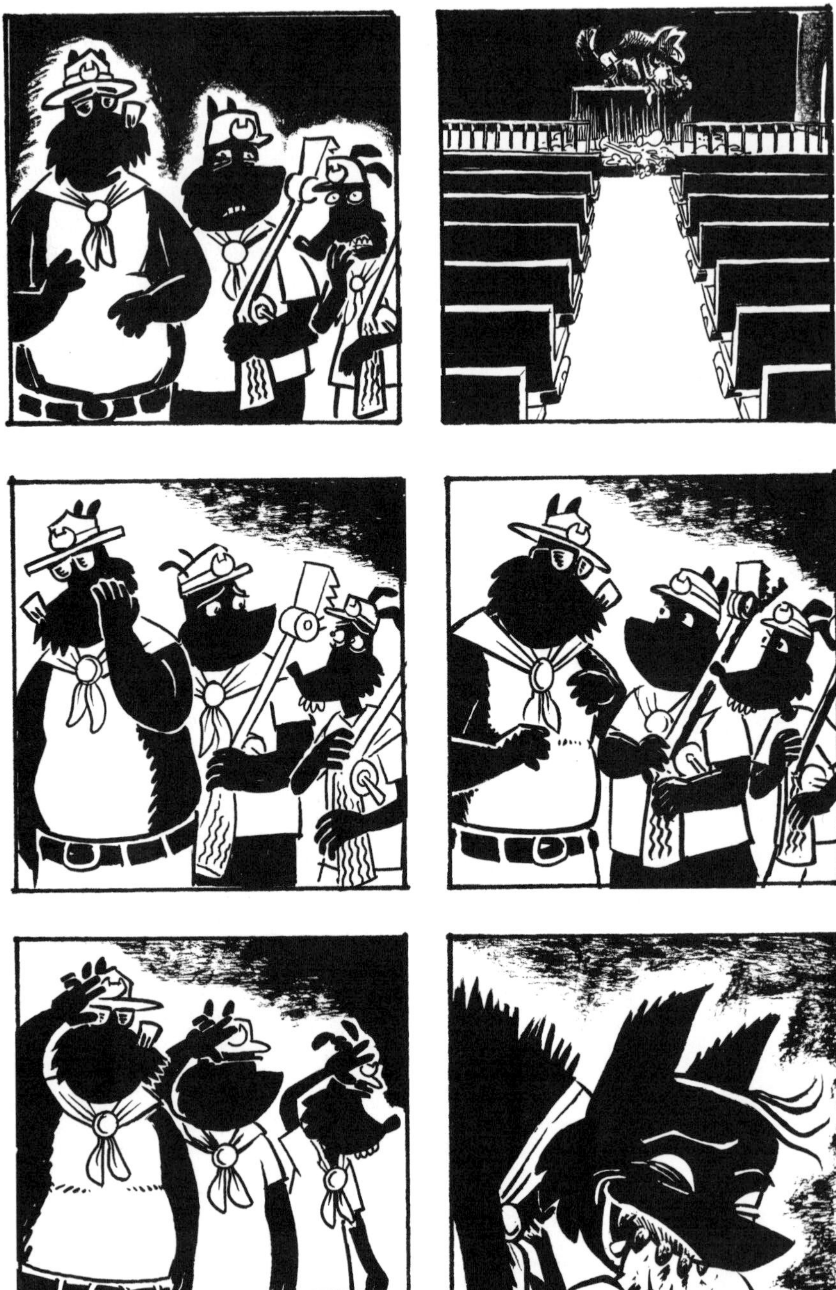

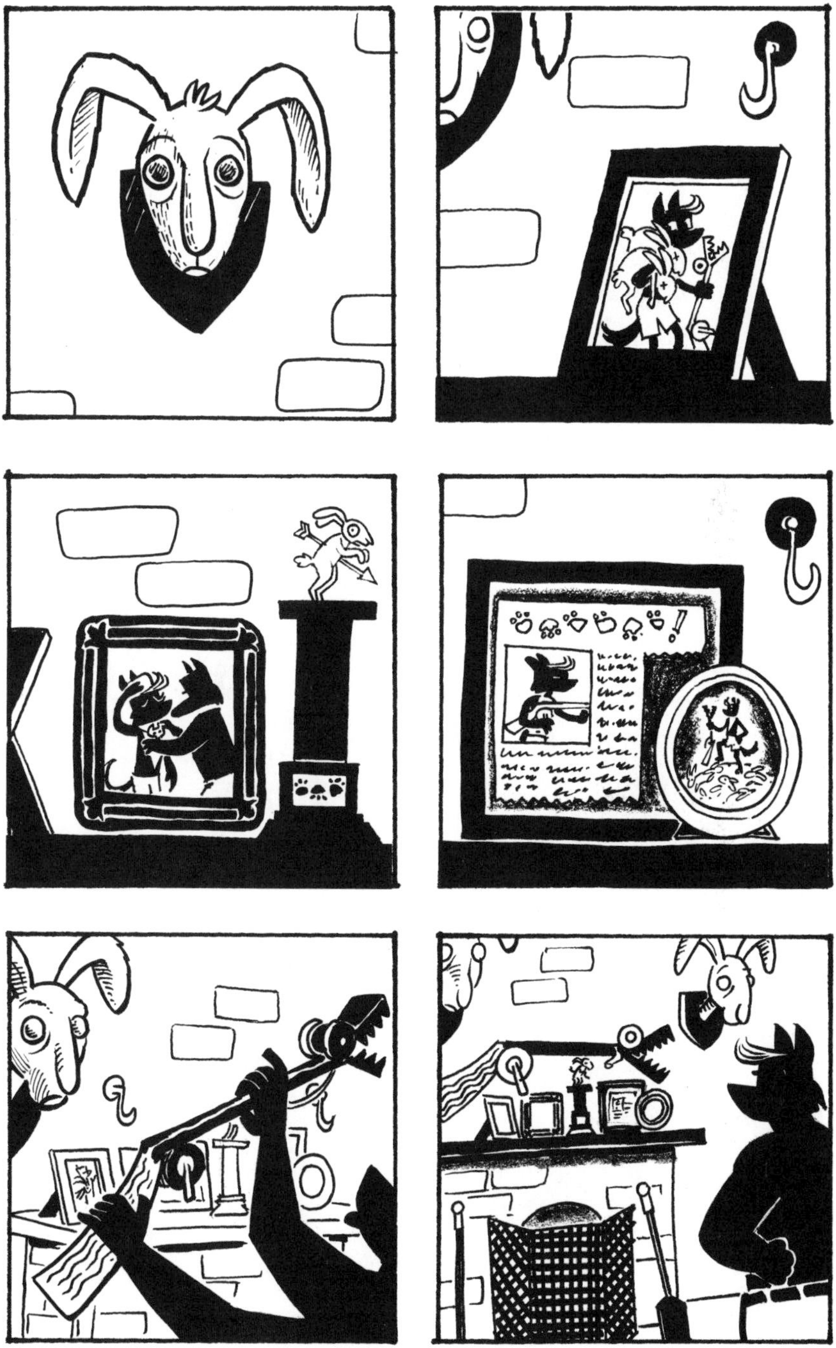

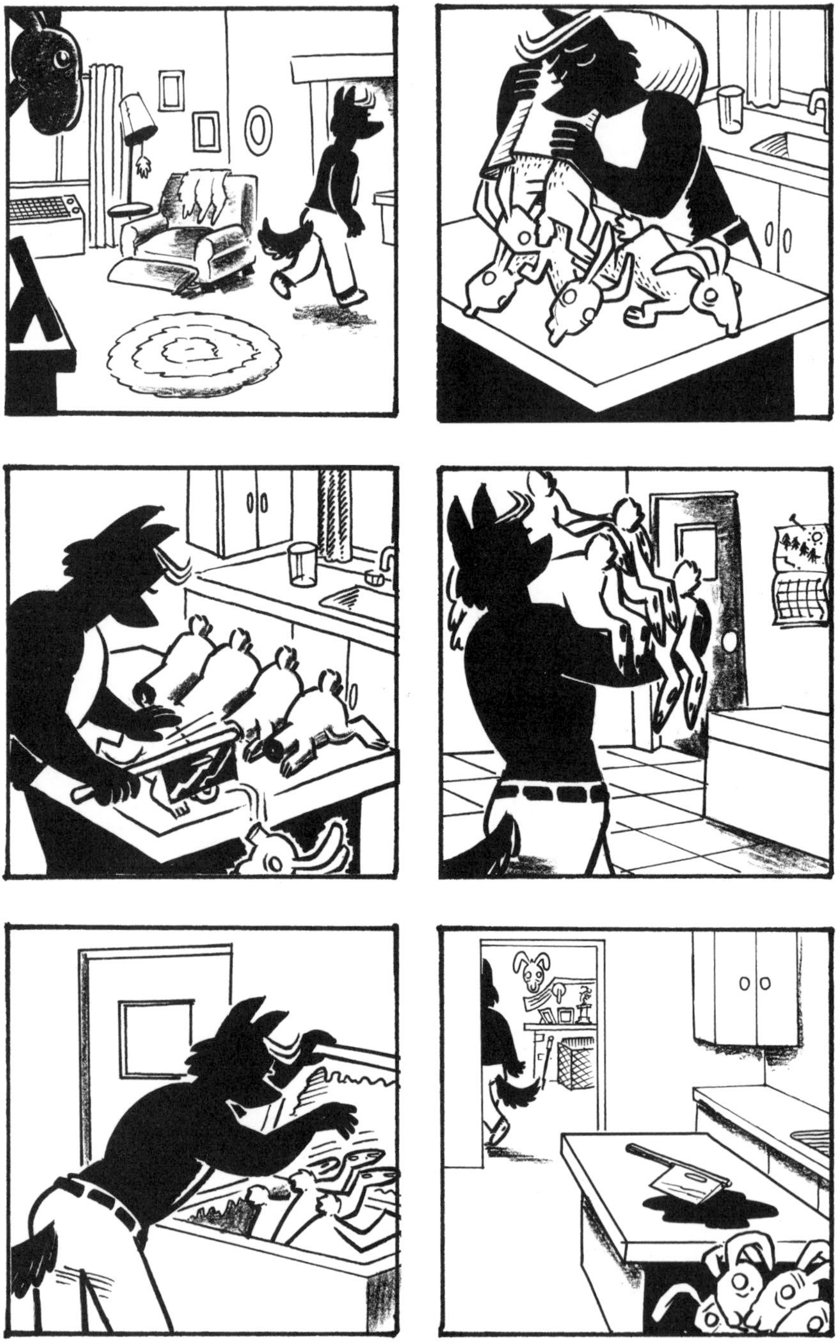

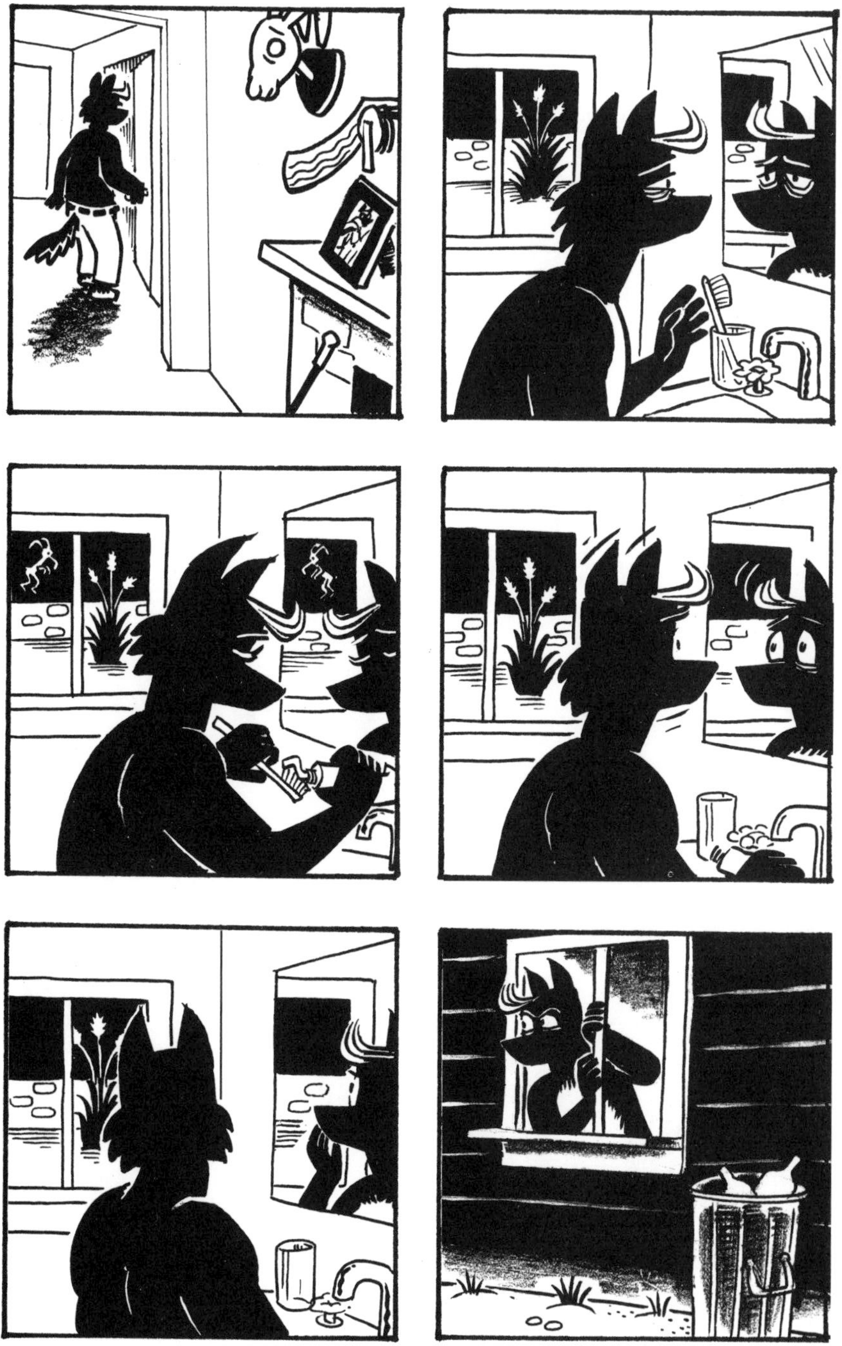

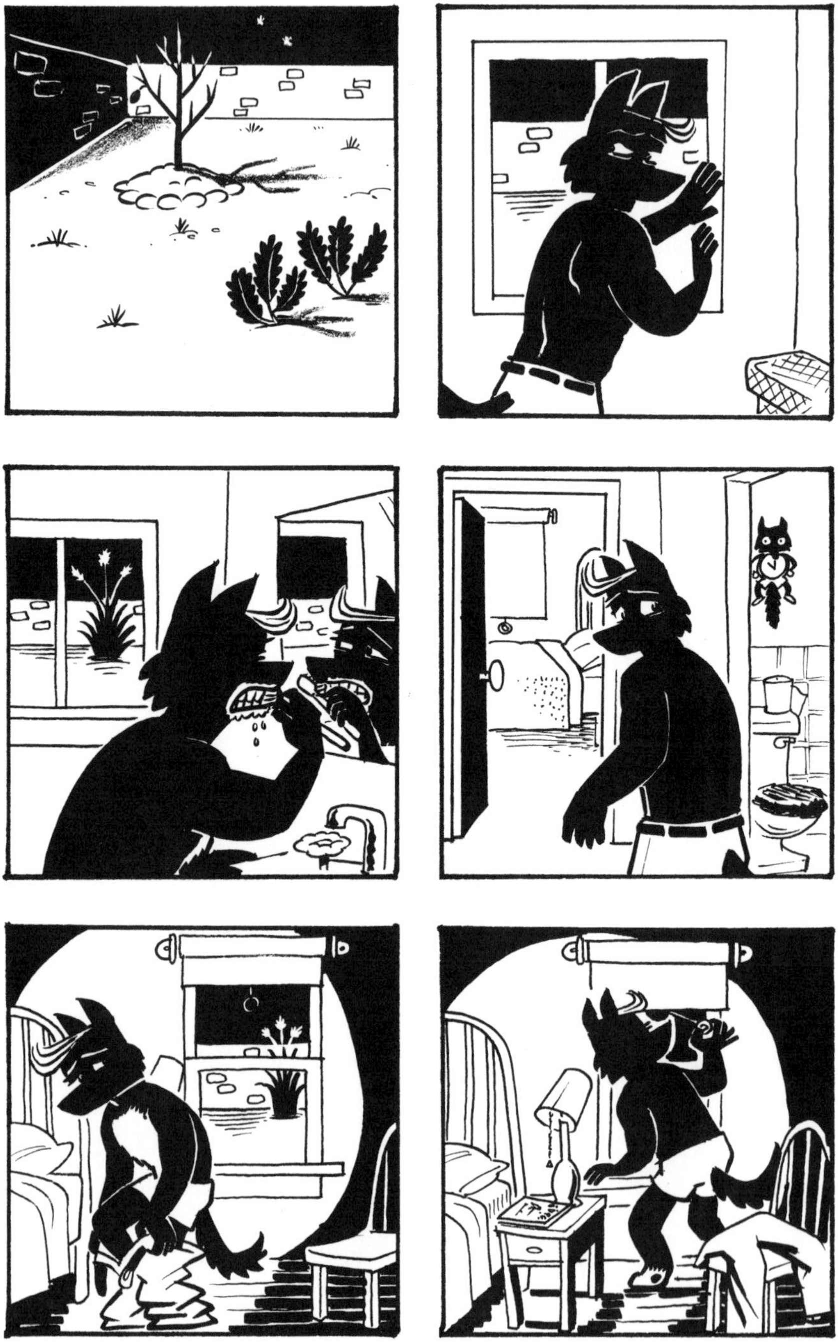

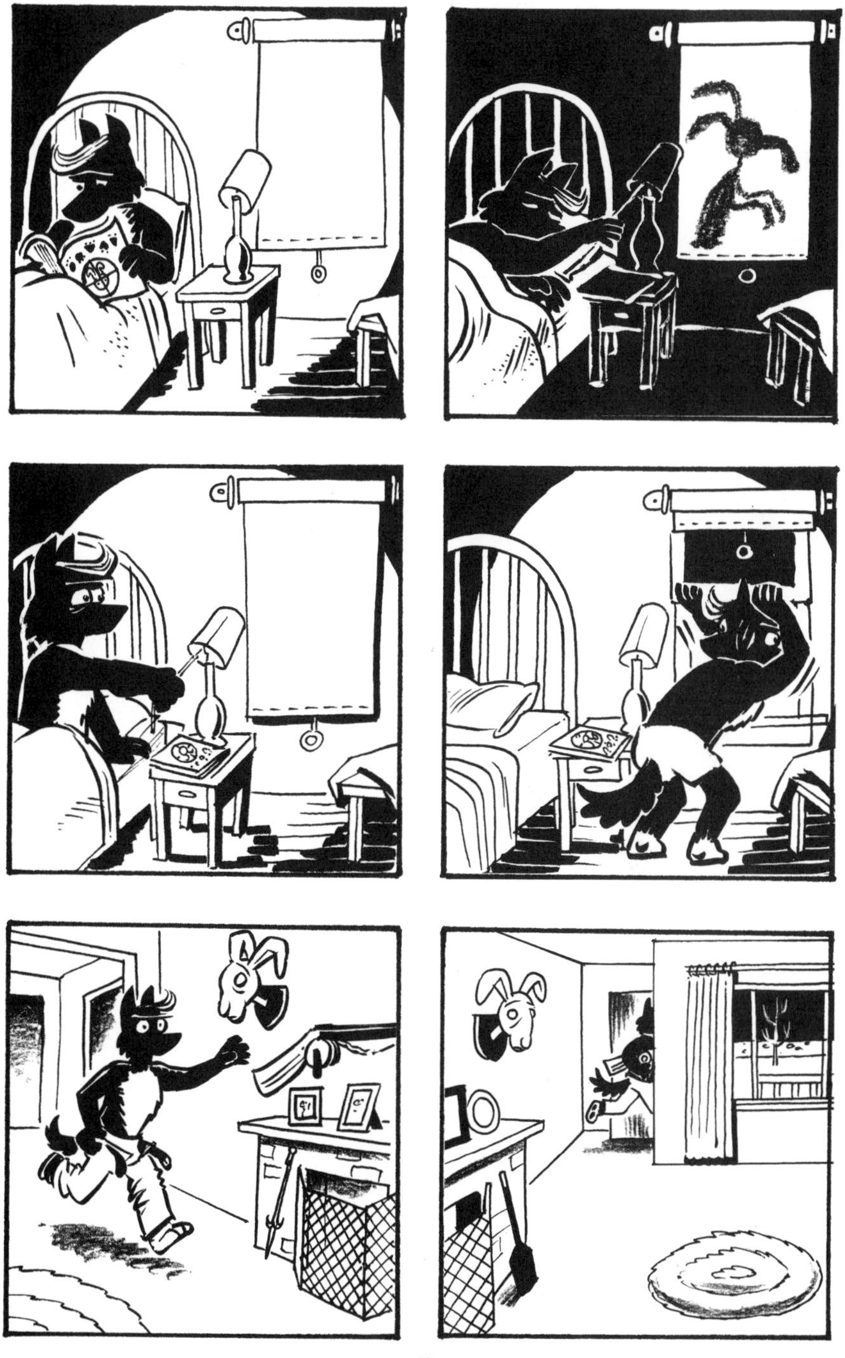

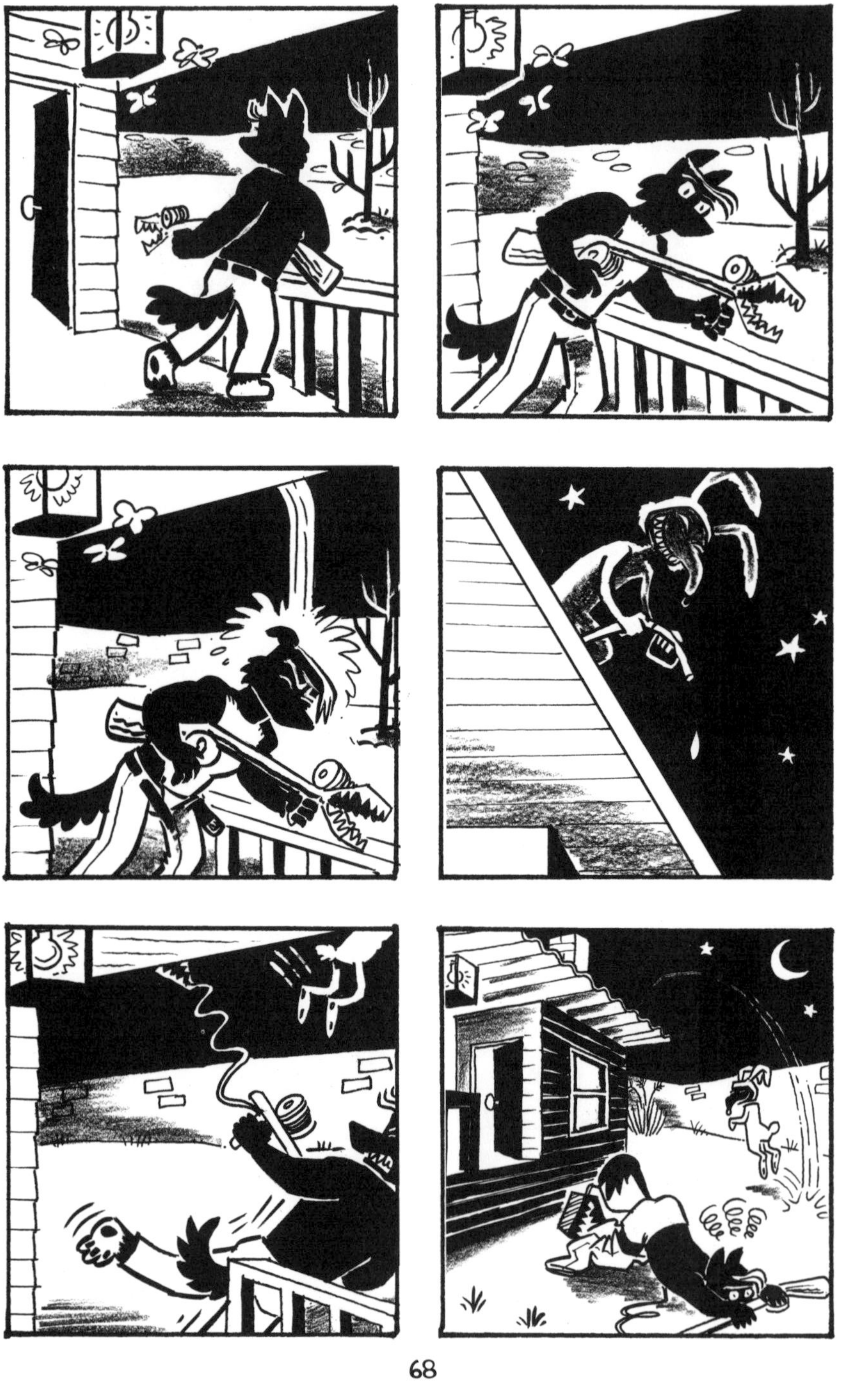

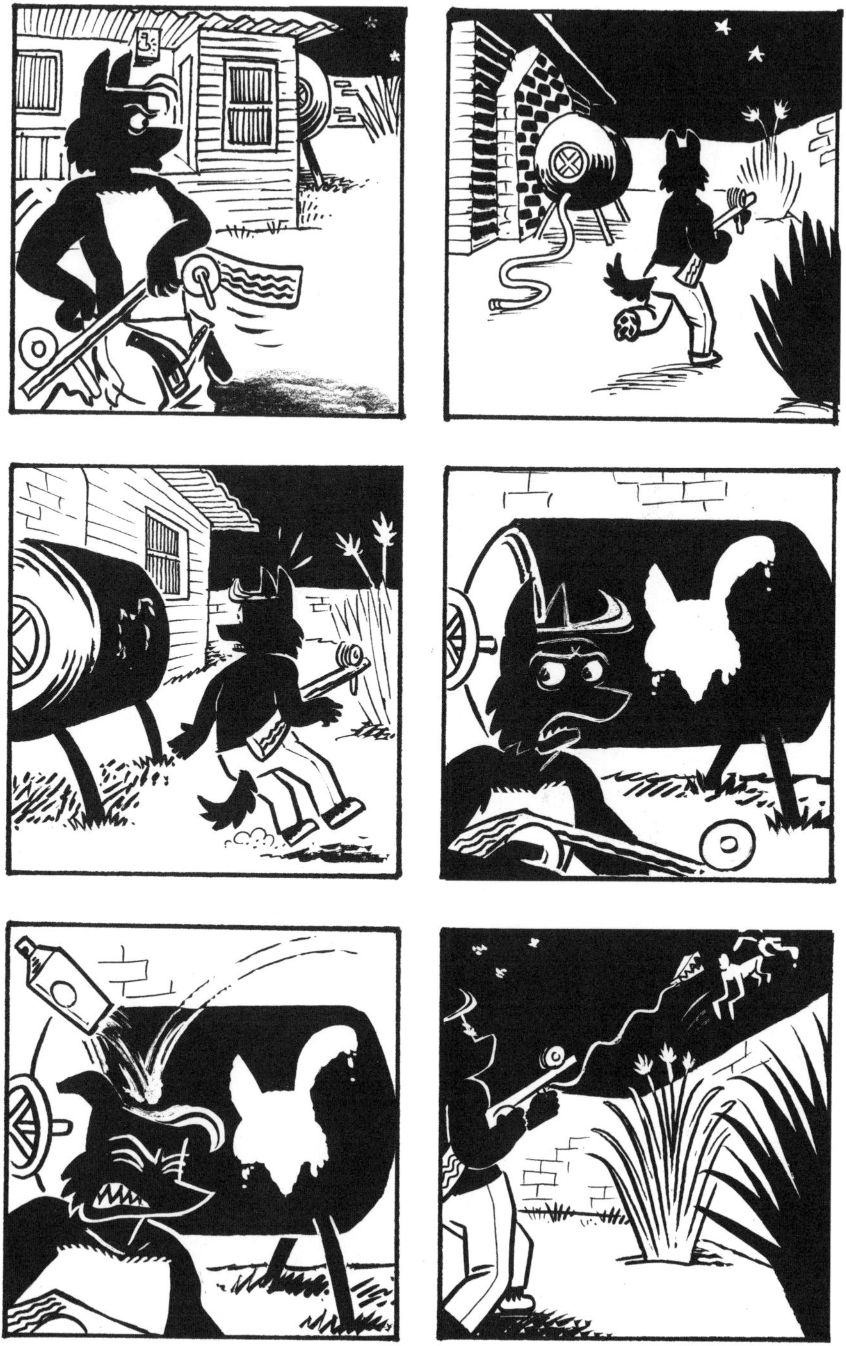

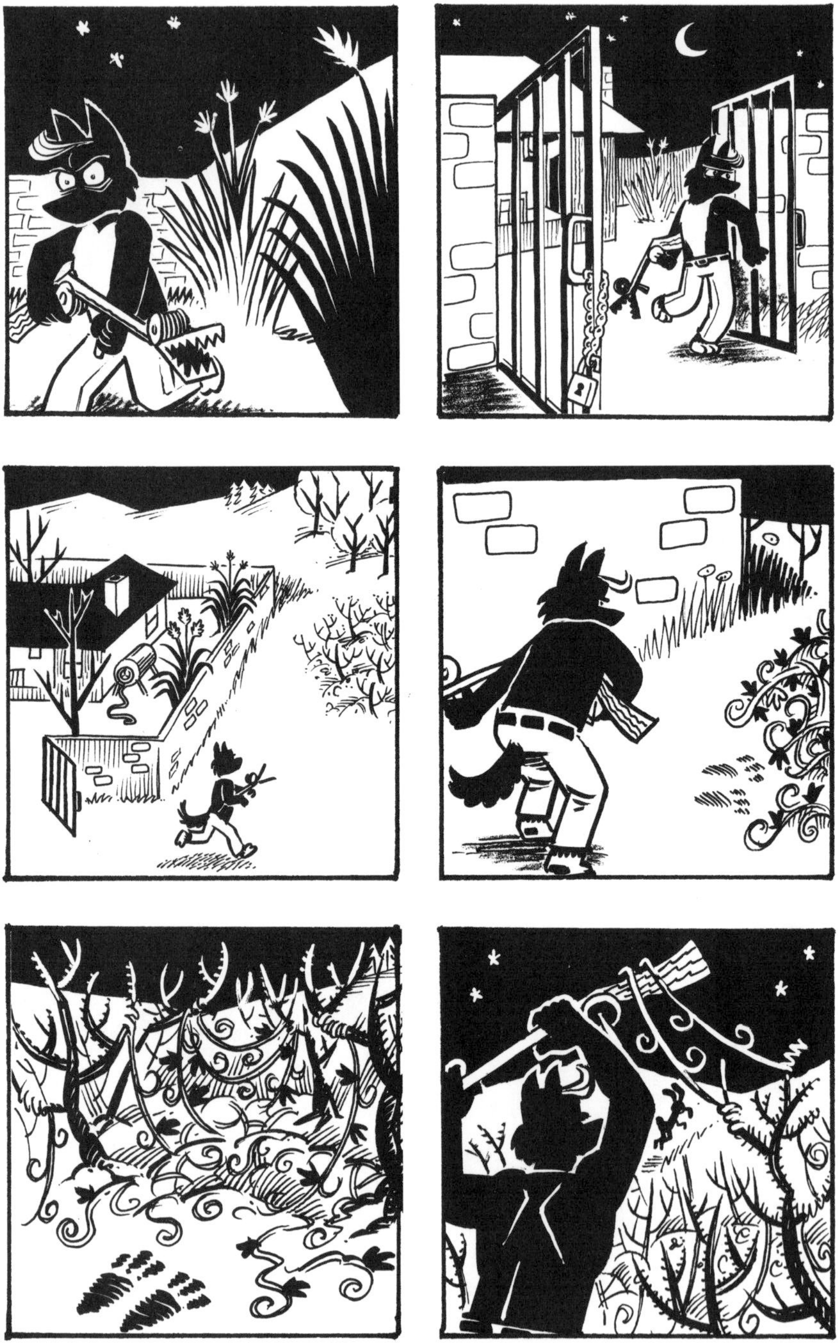

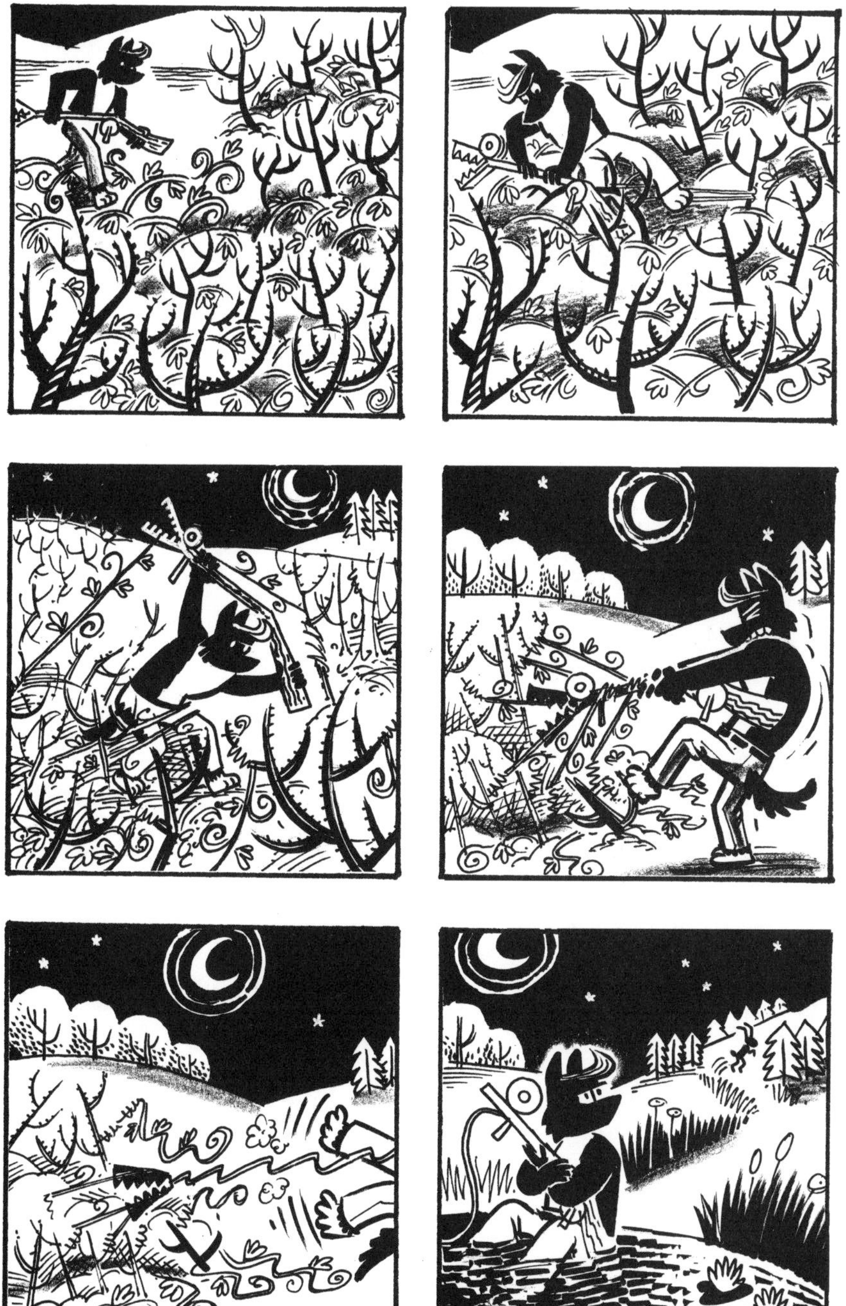

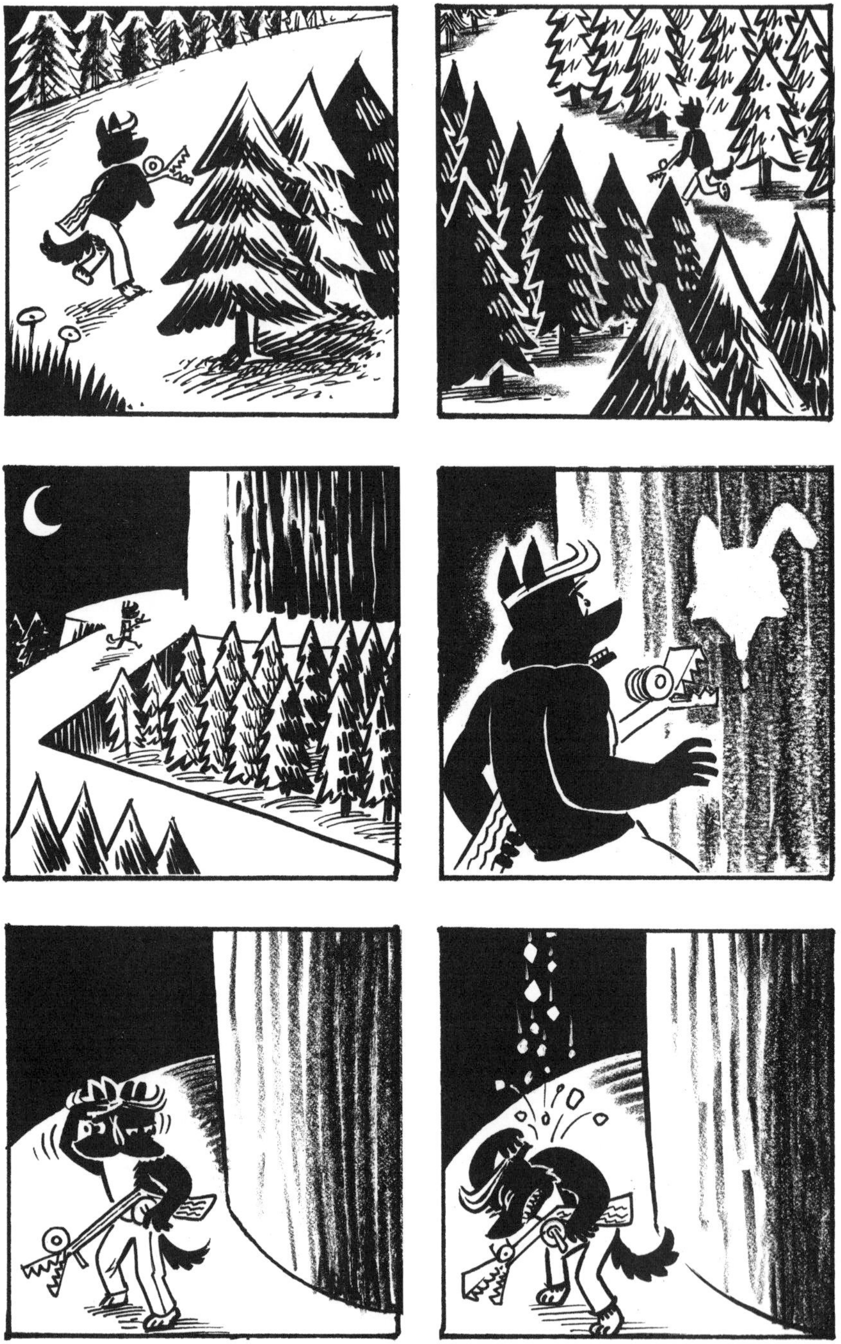

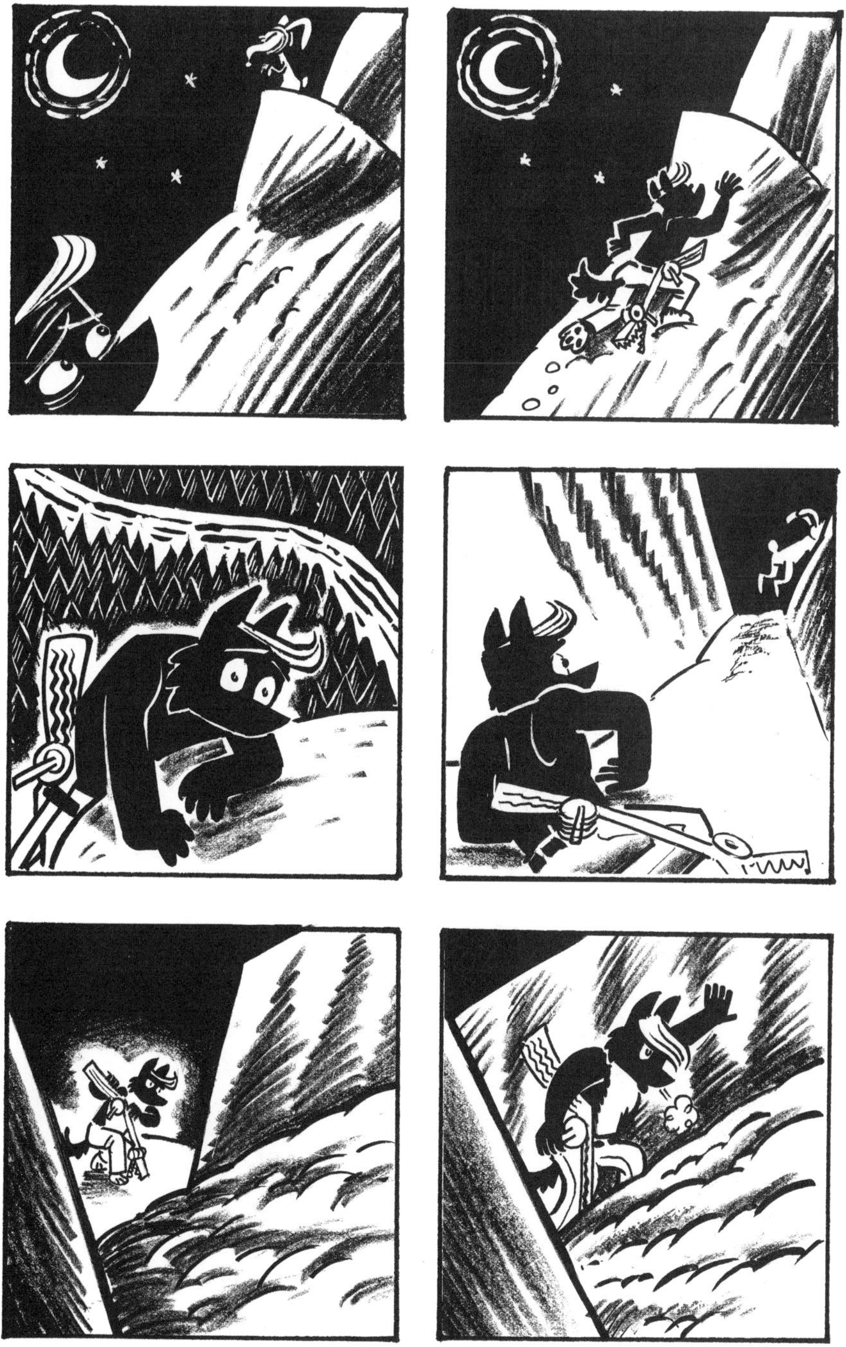

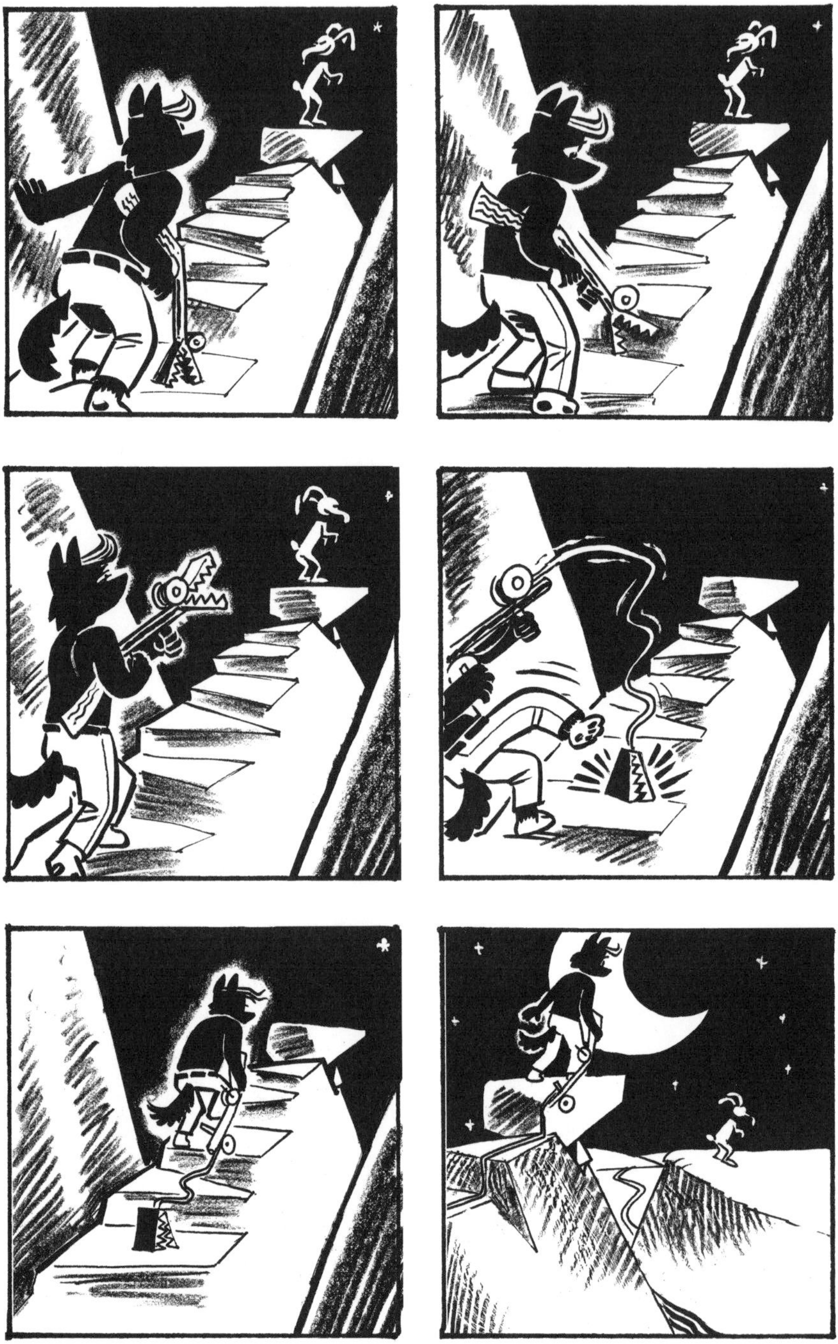

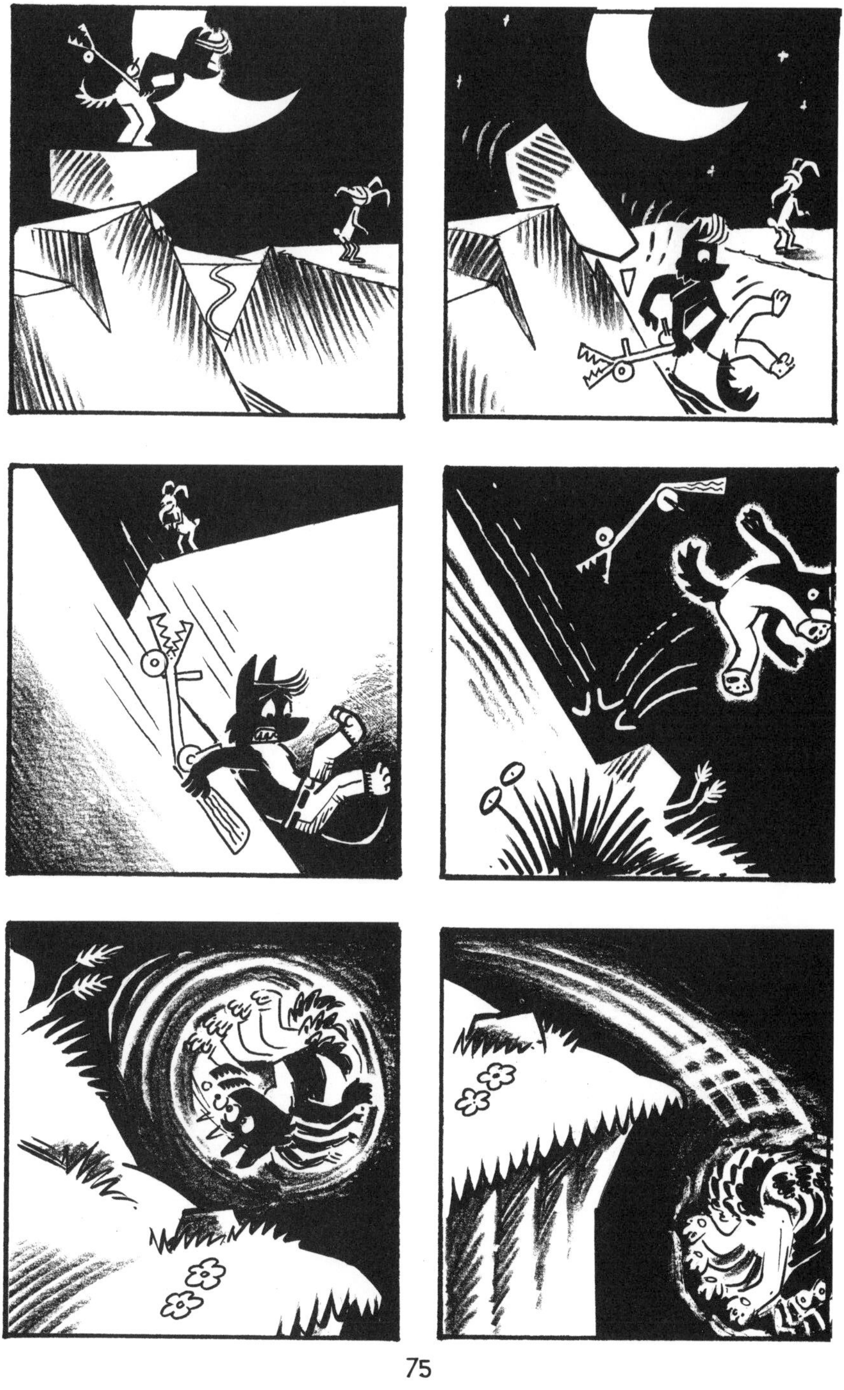

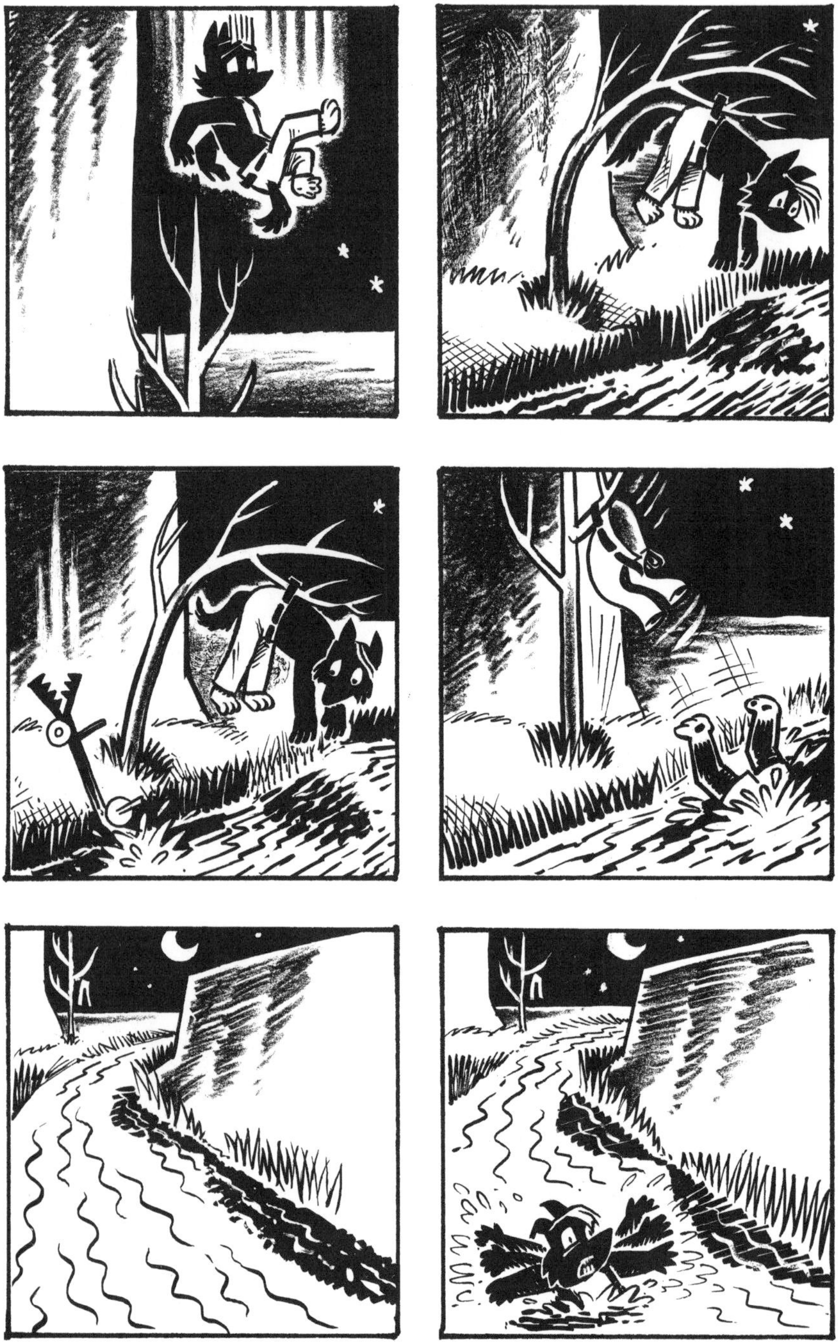

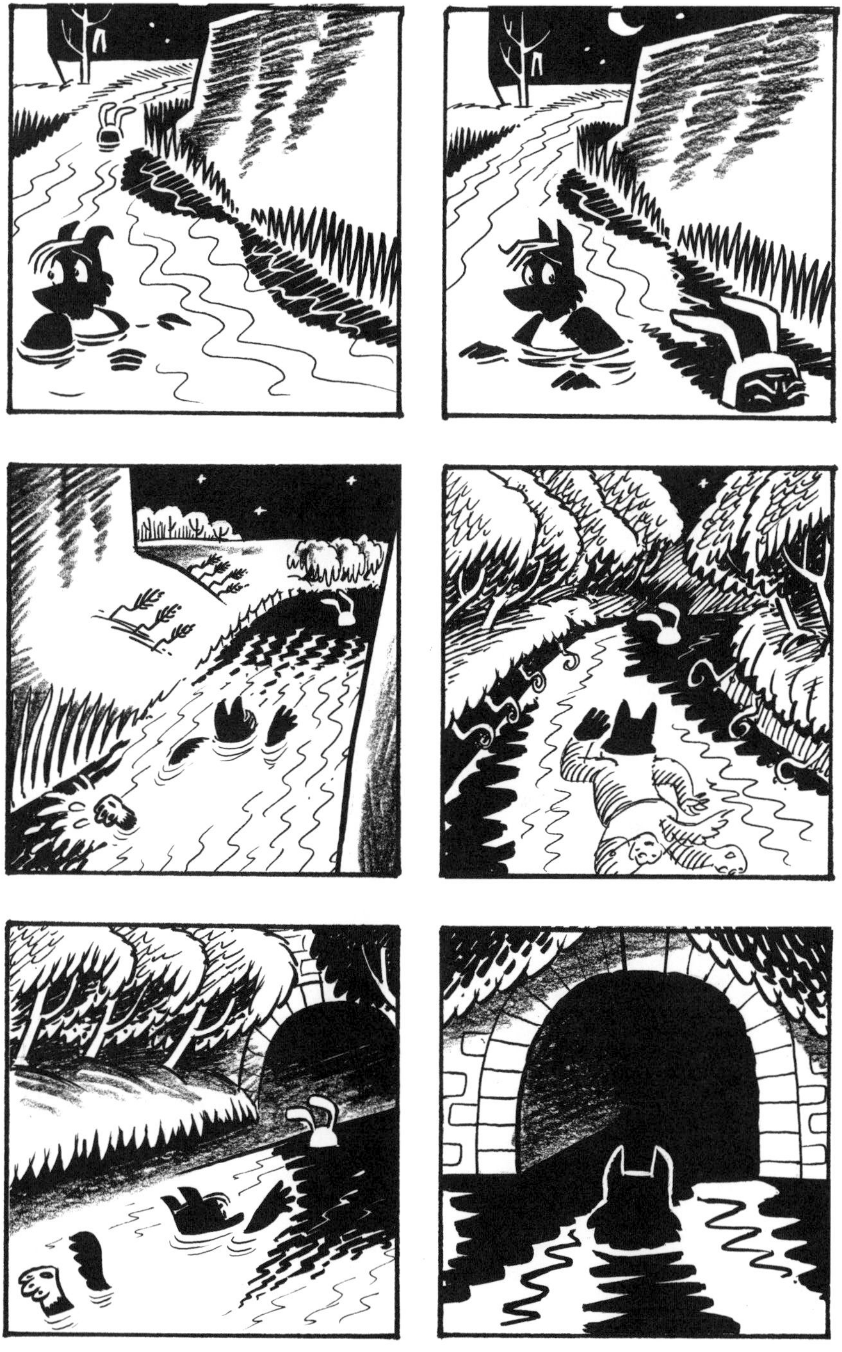

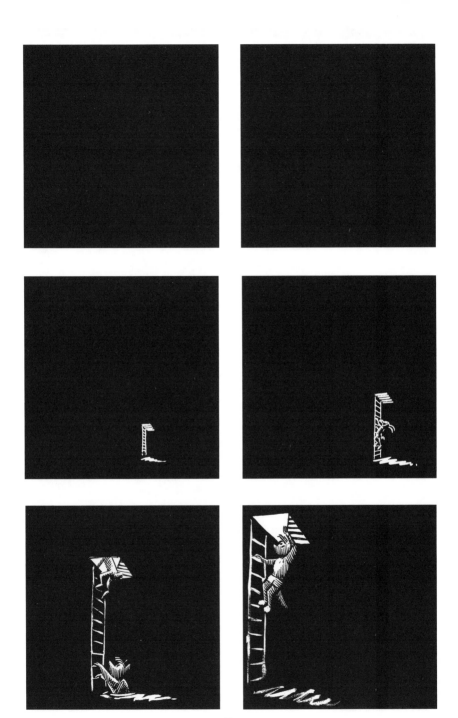

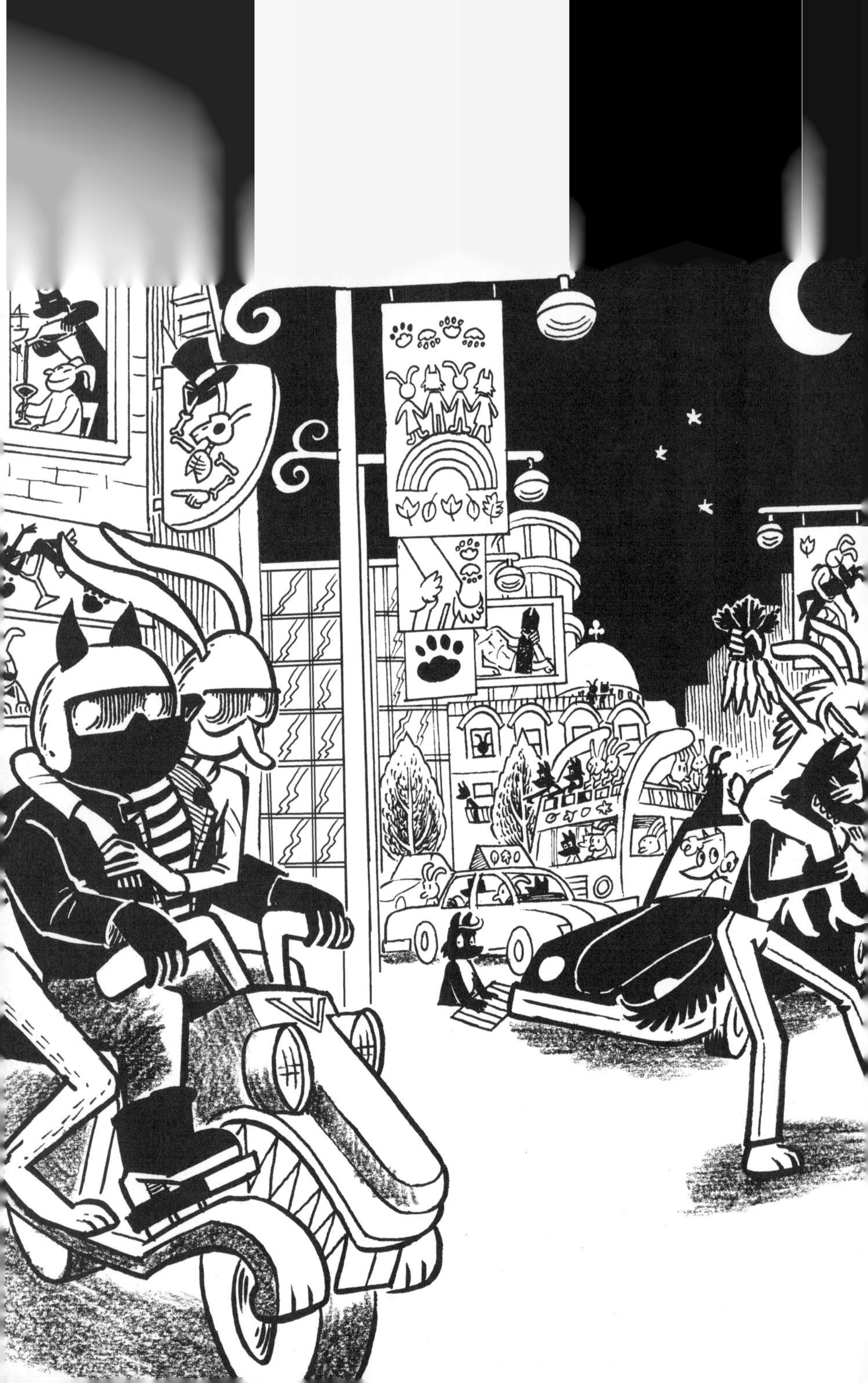

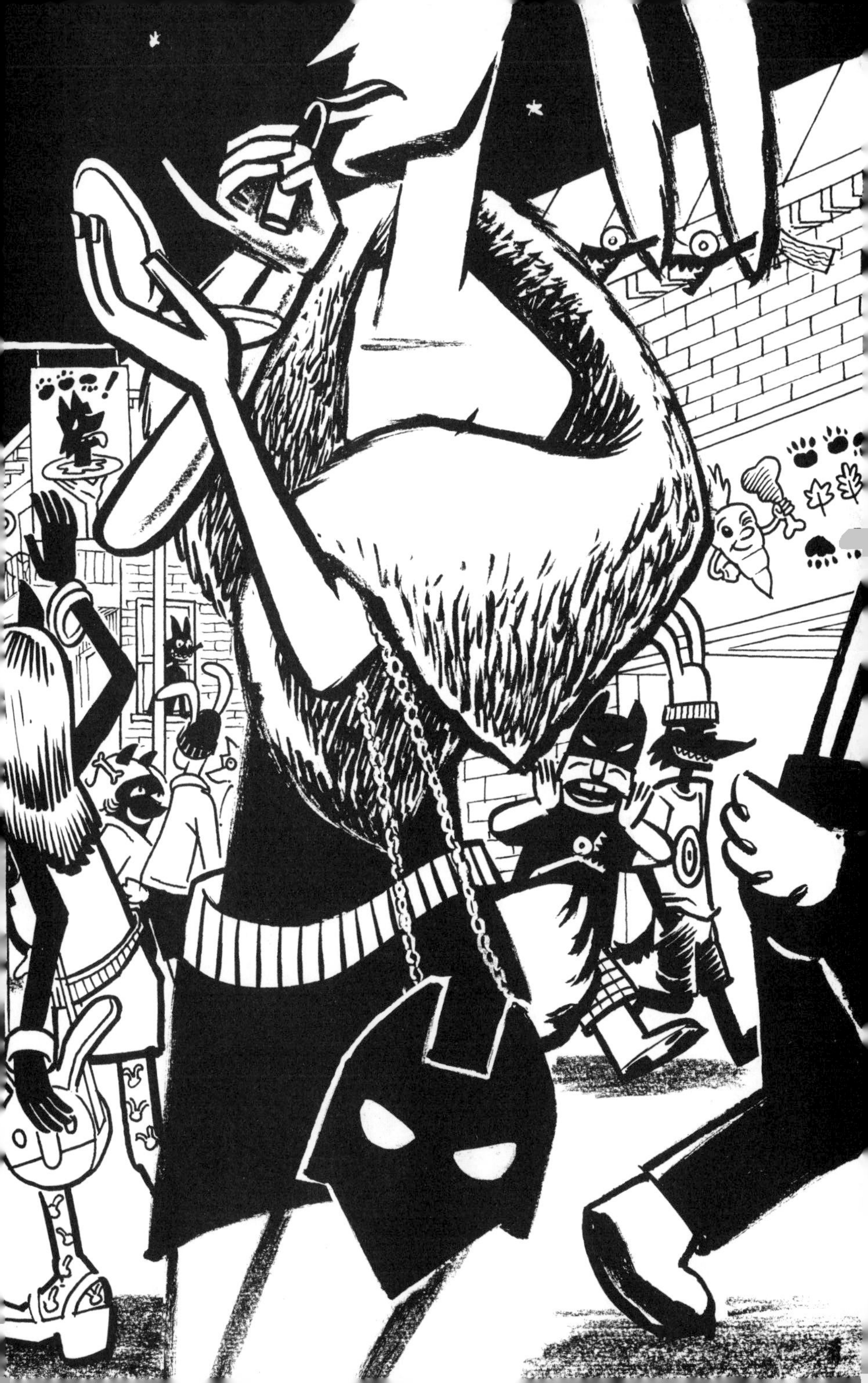

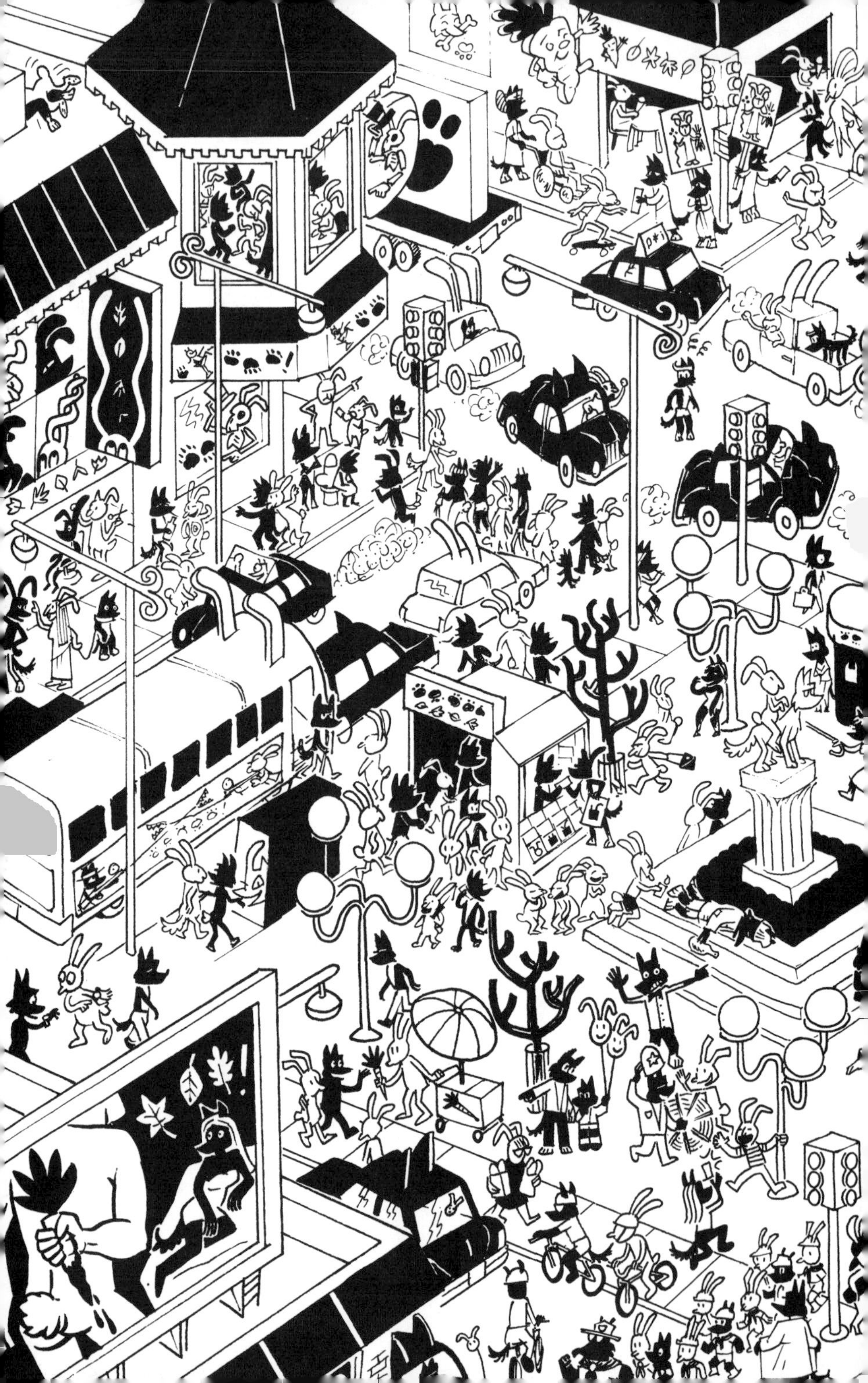

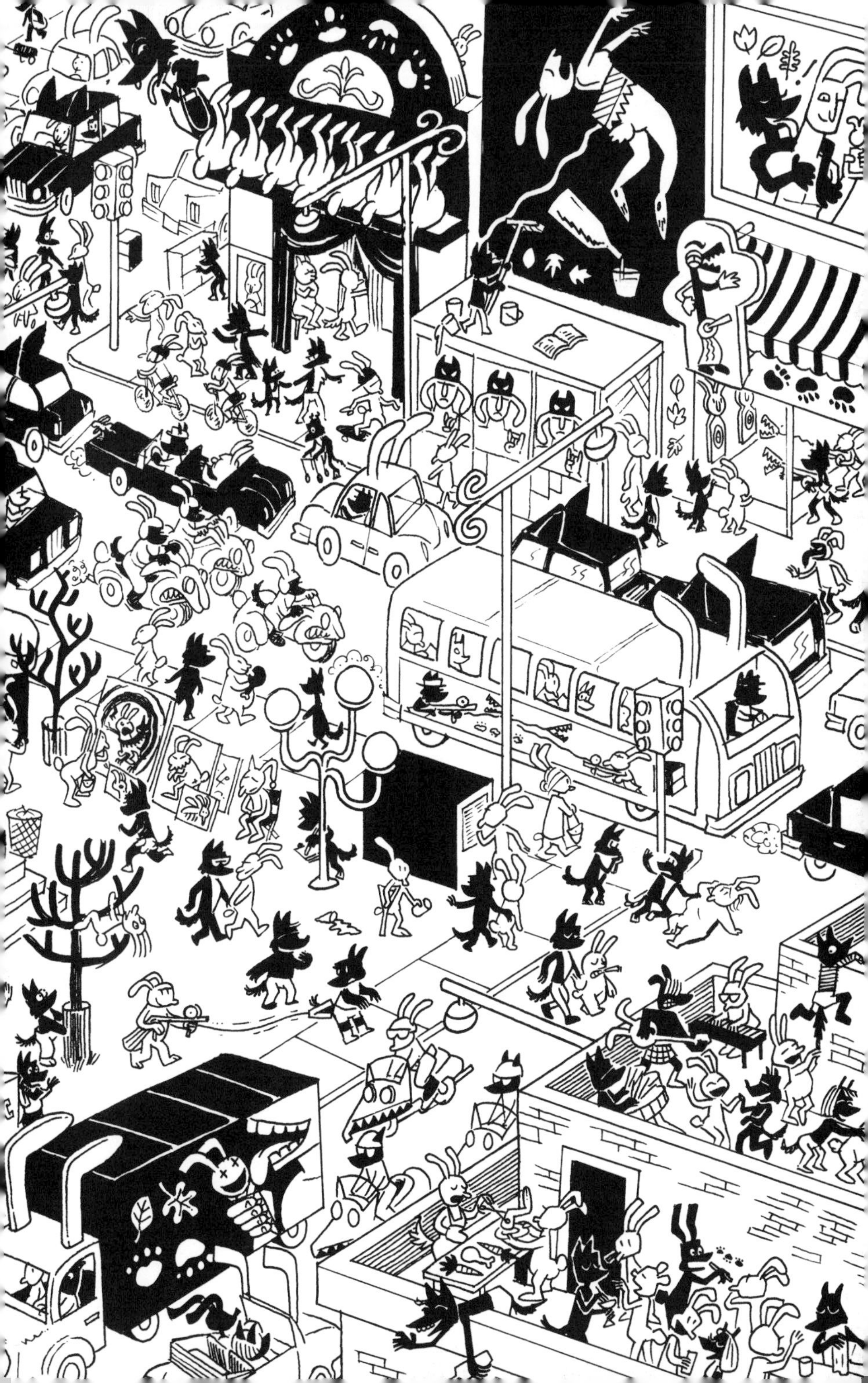

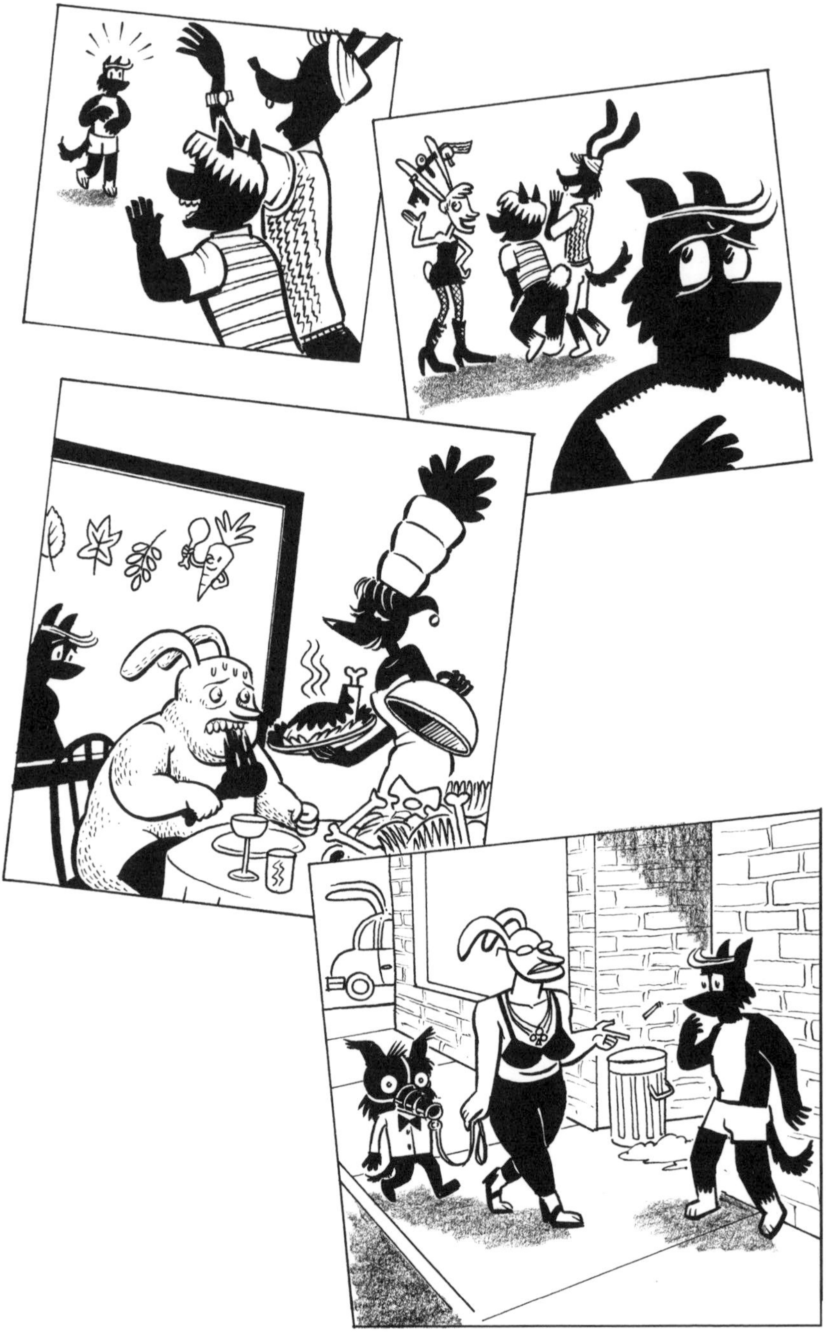

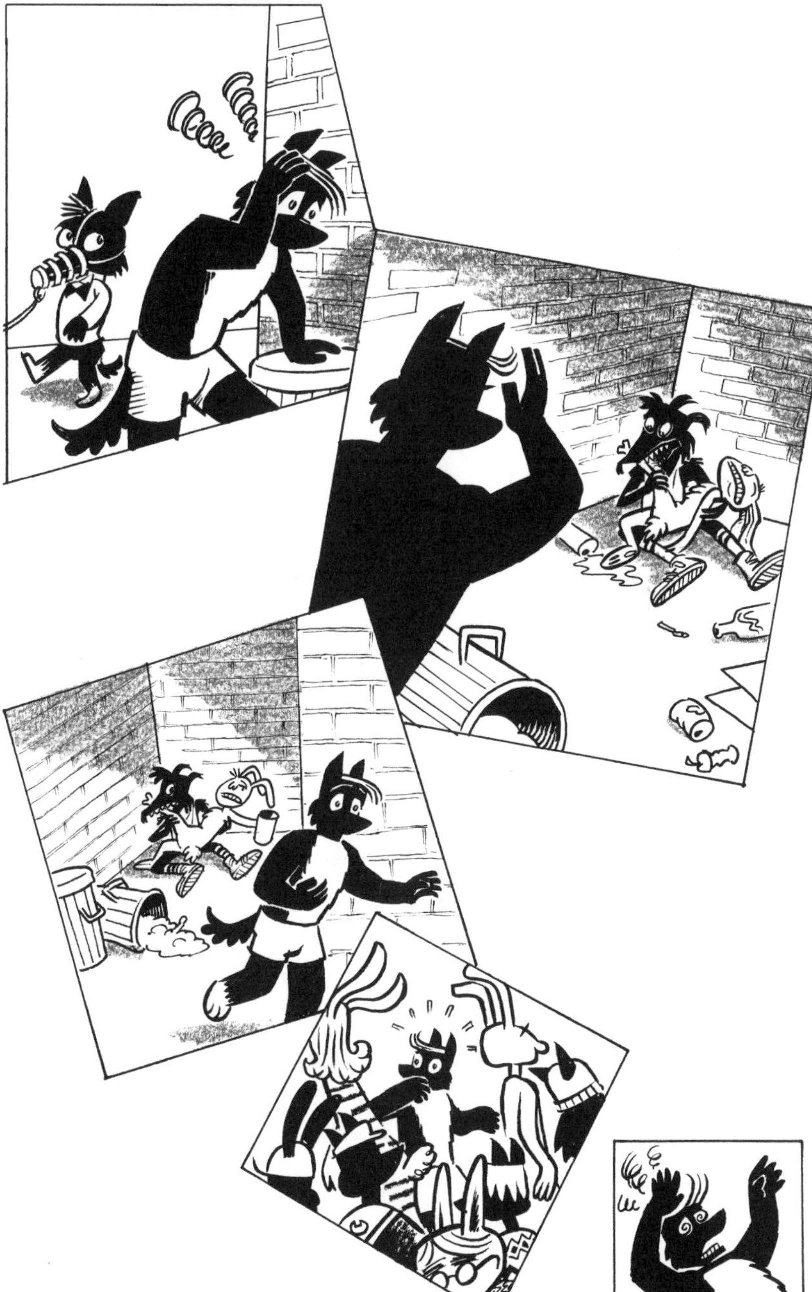

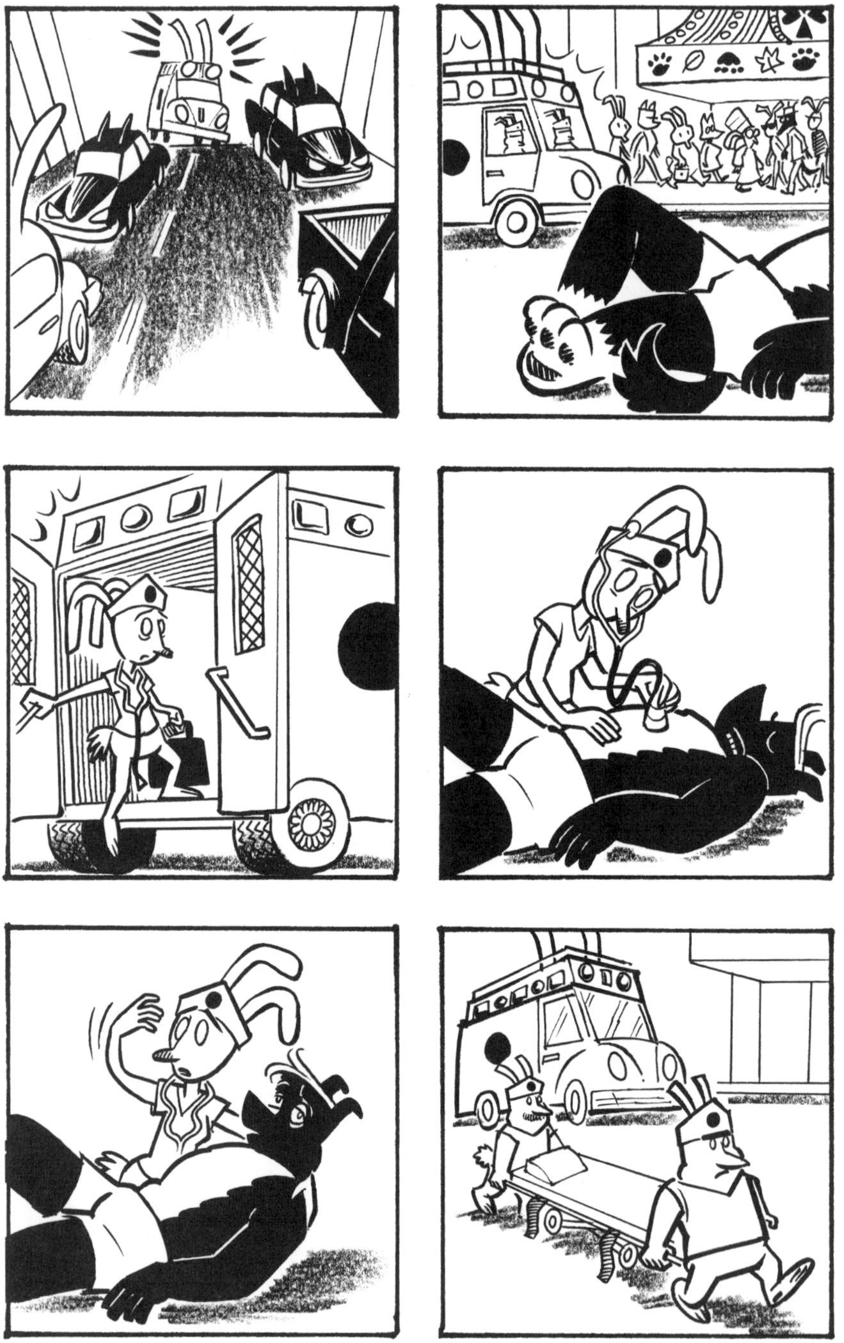

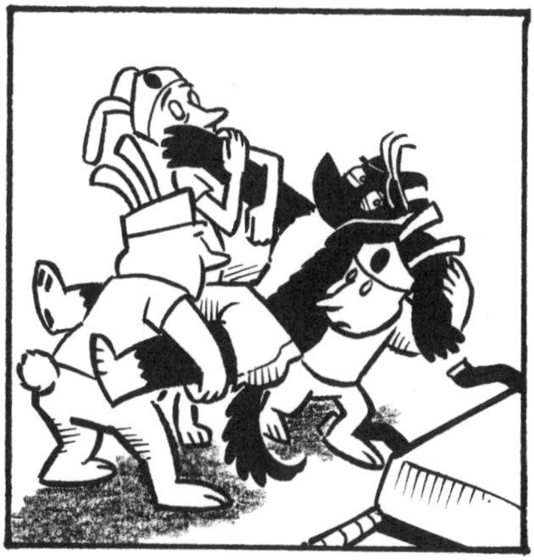
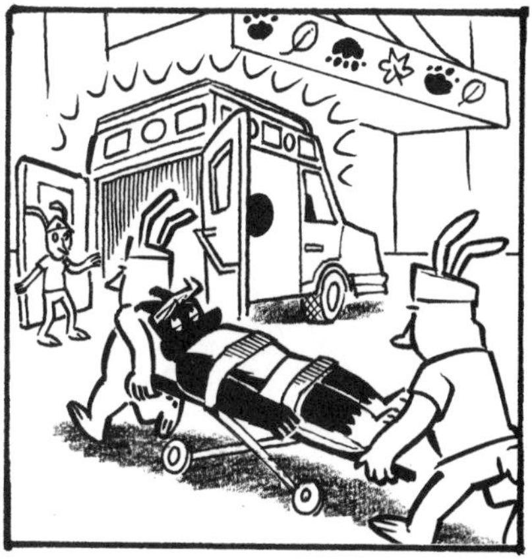
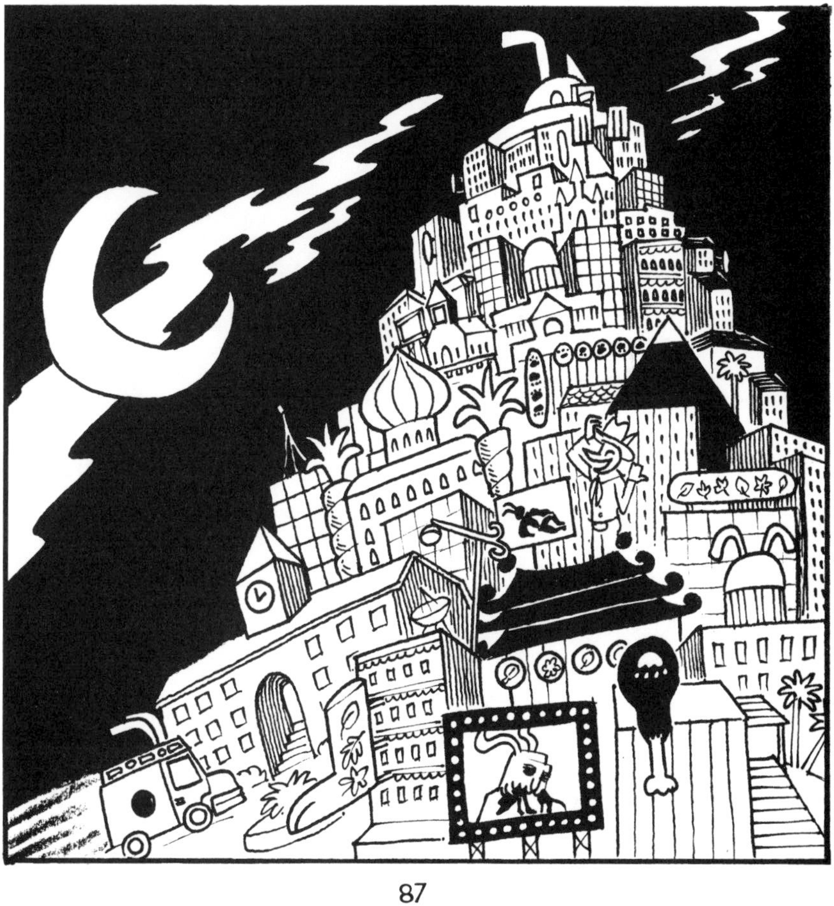

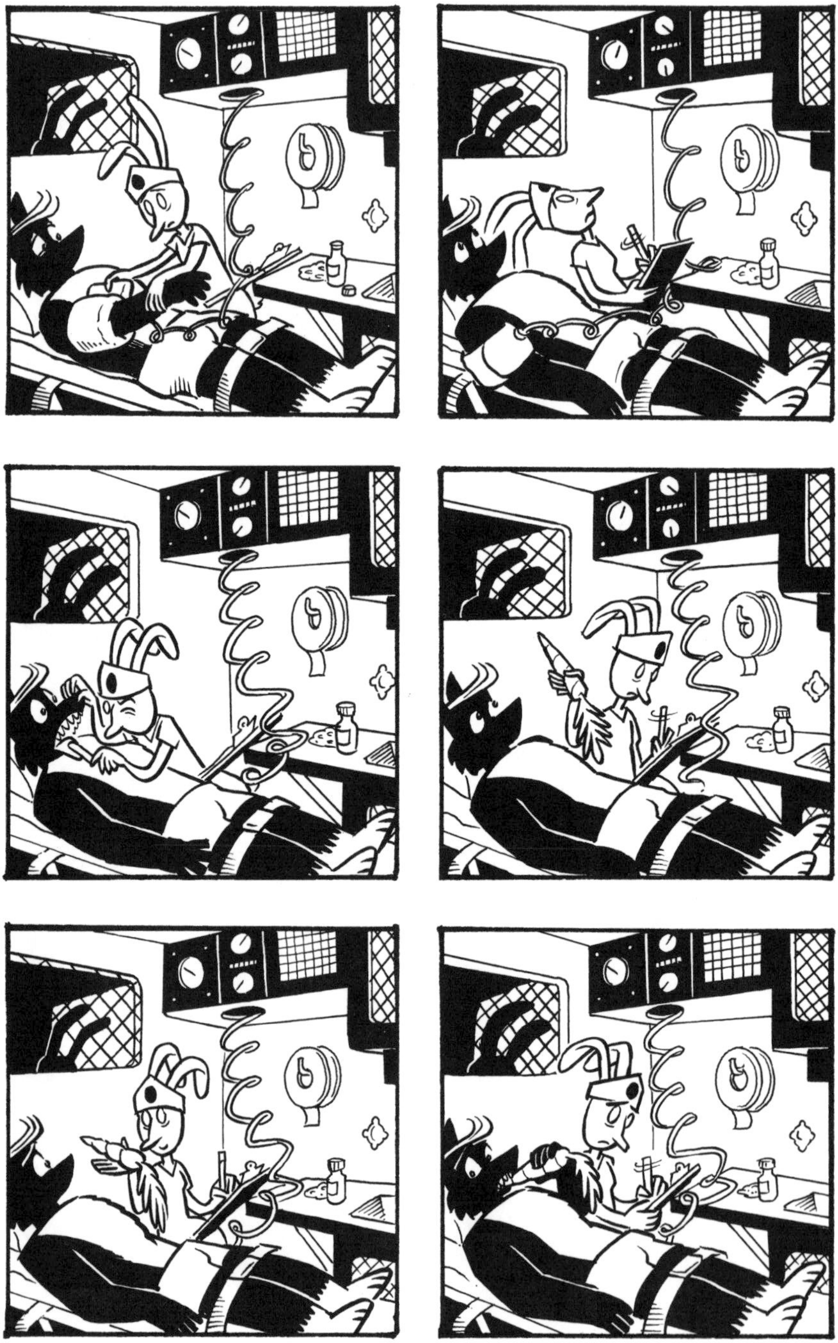

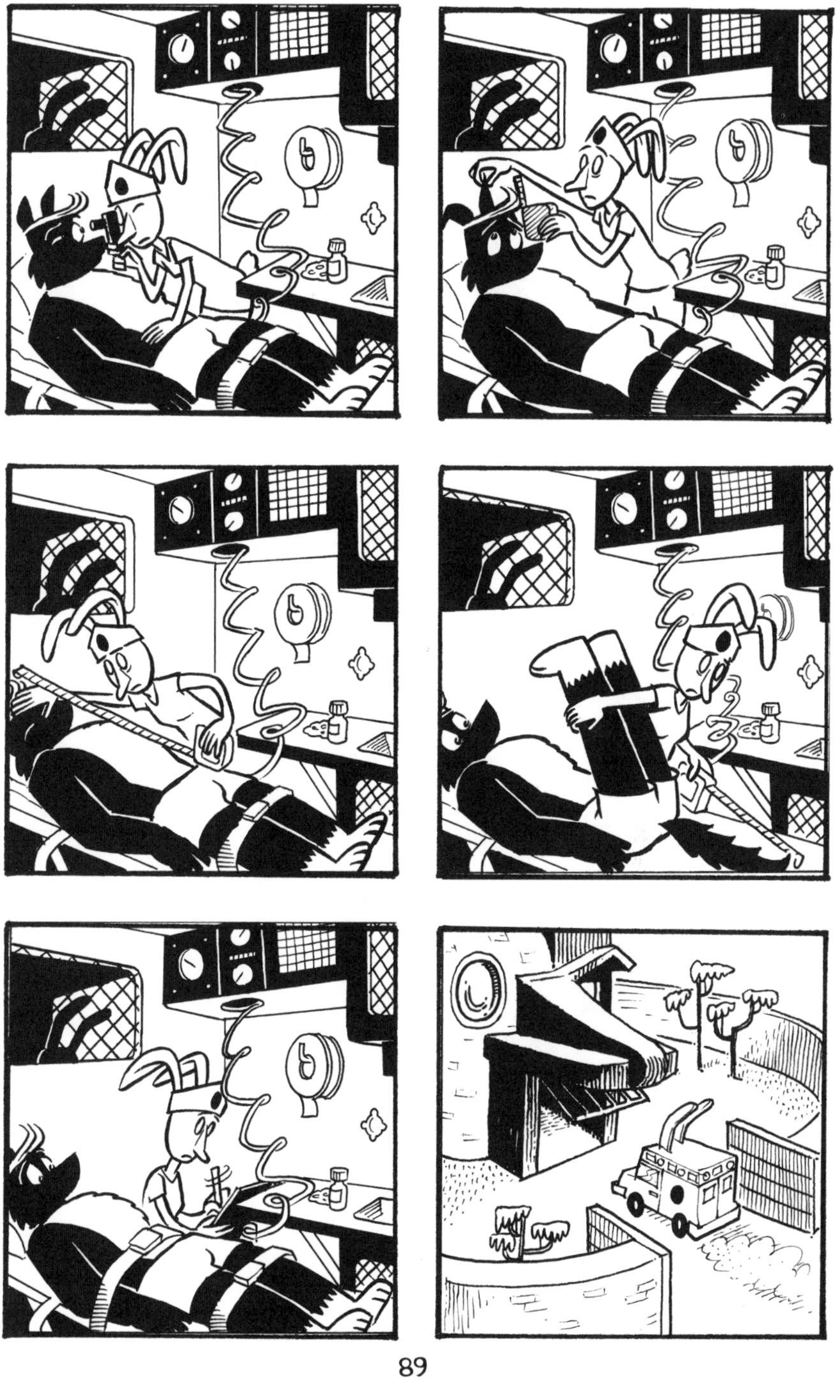

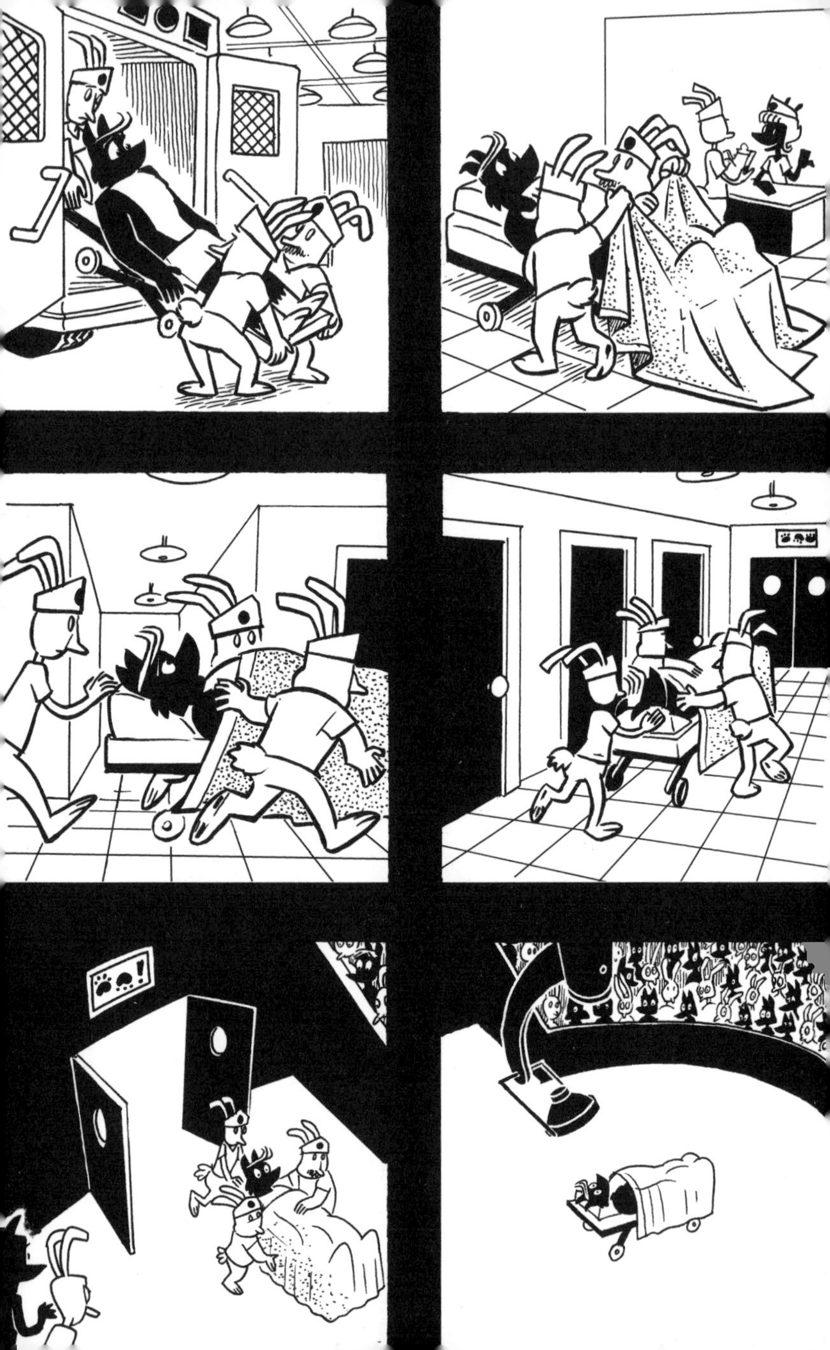

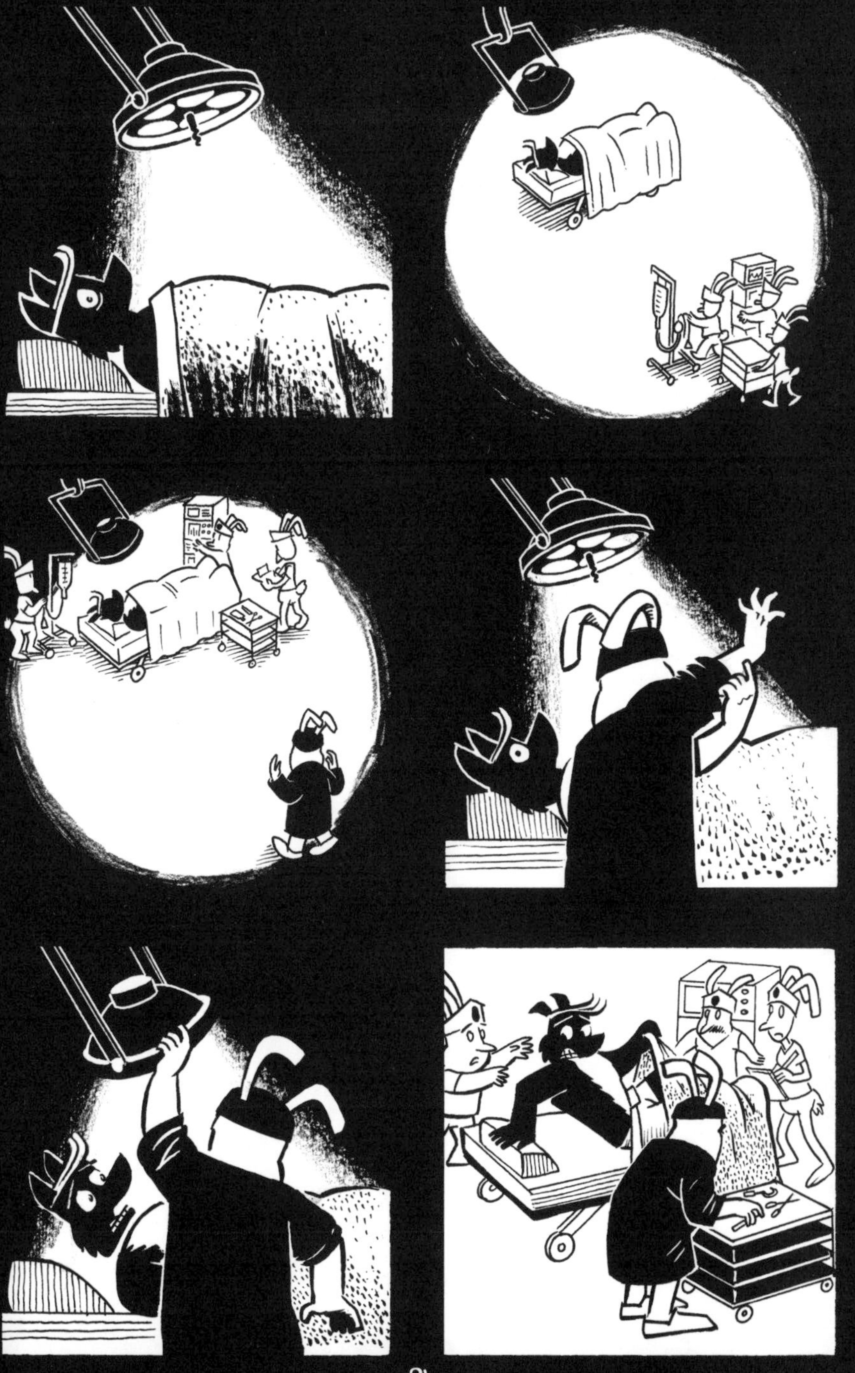

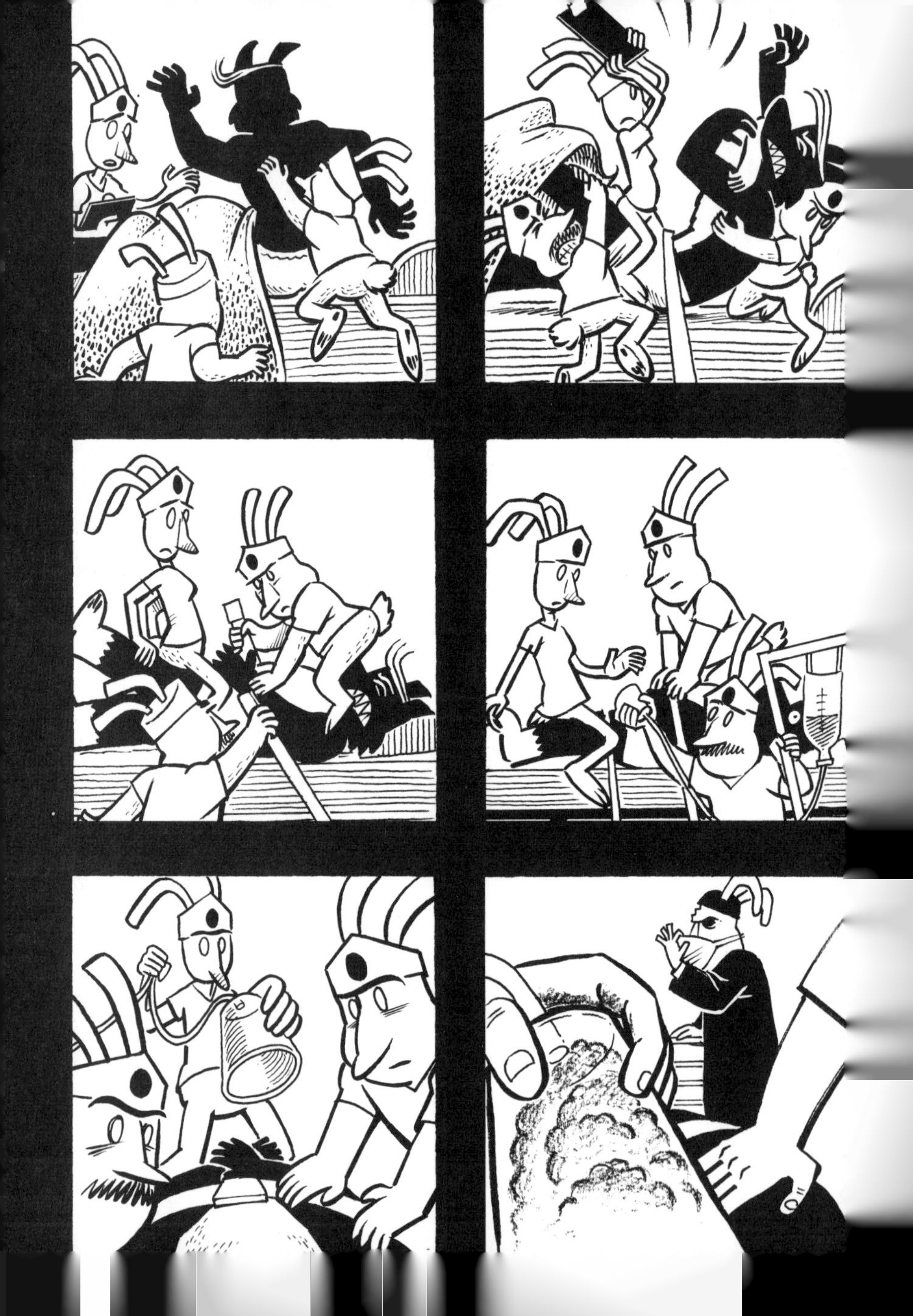

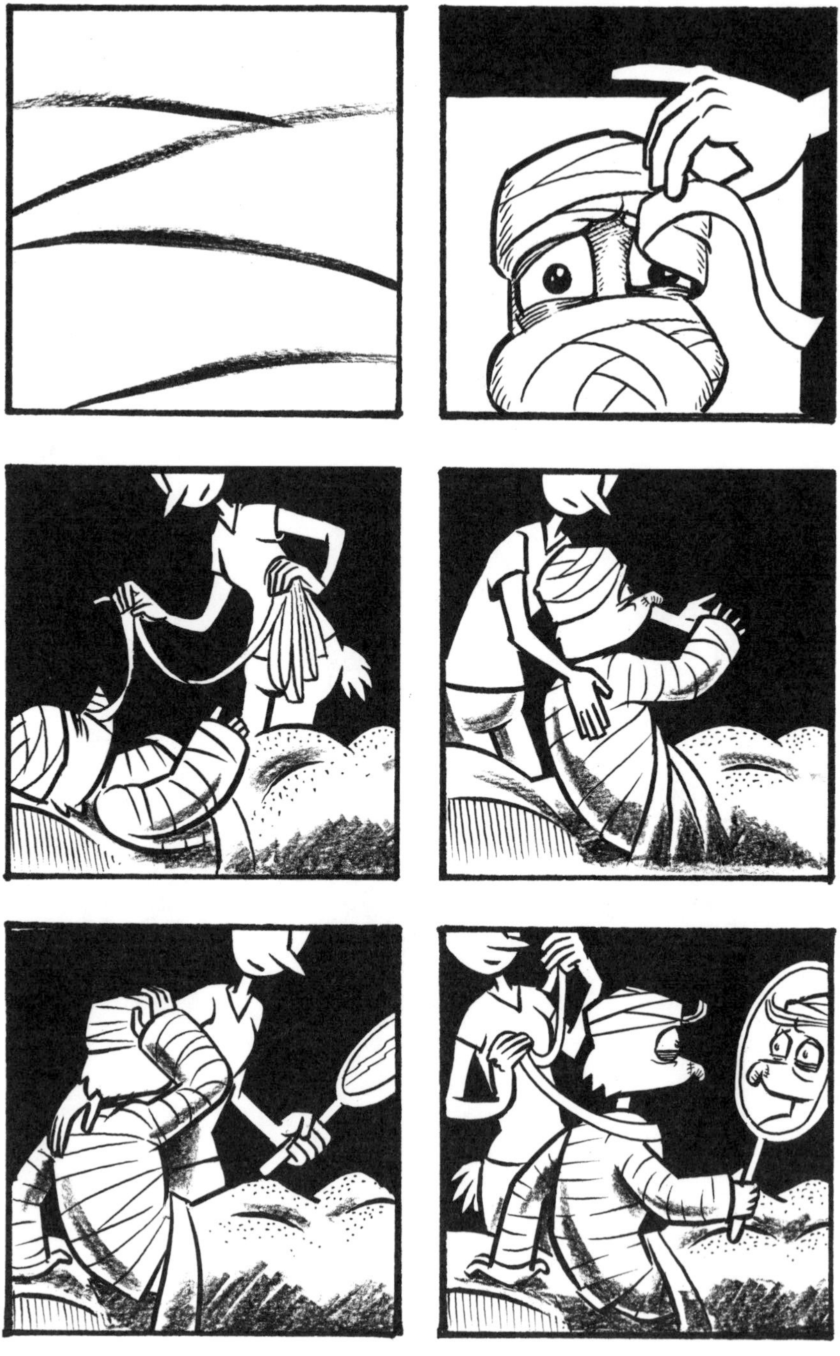

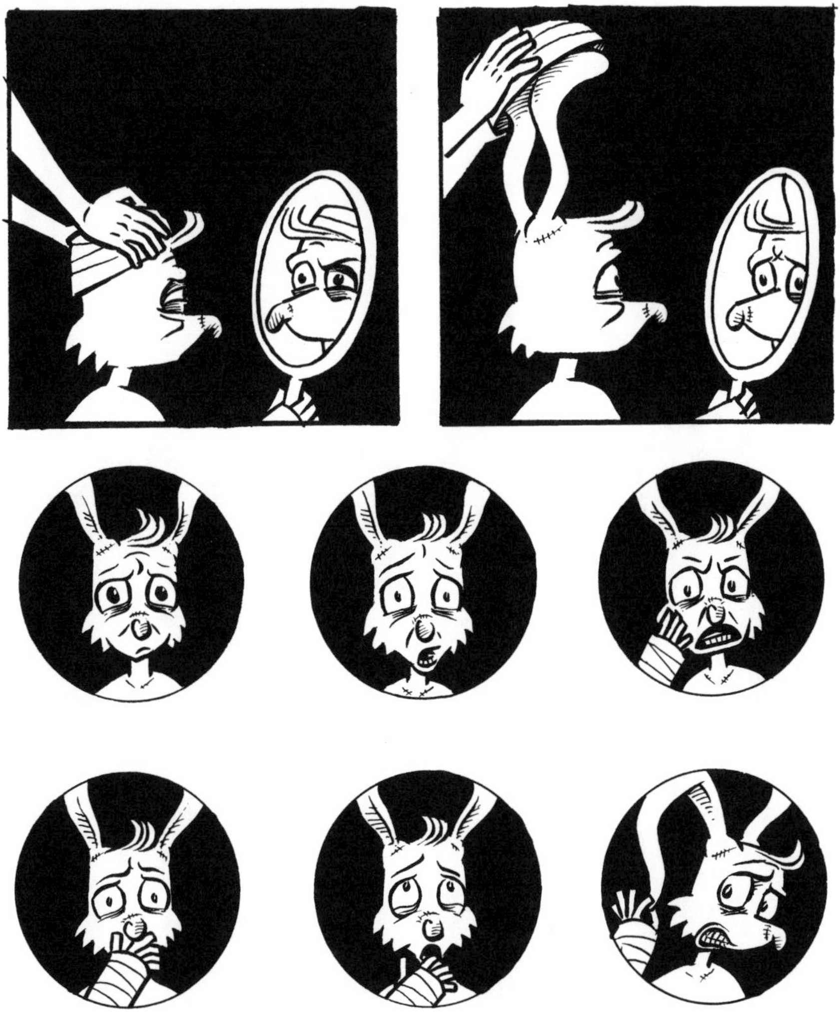

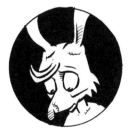

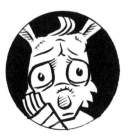

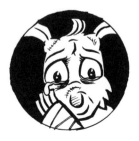

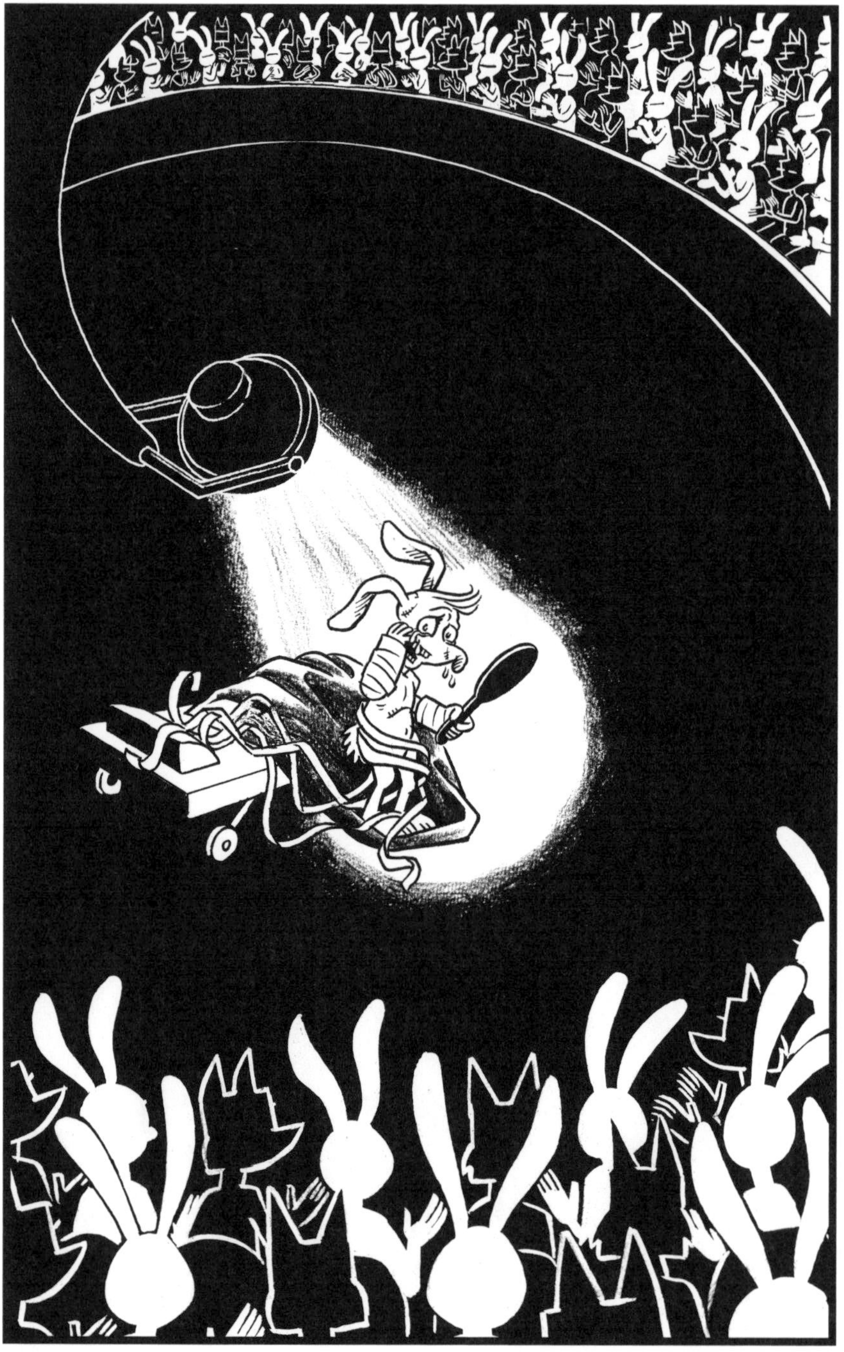

Special thanks to
Erik Nebel, Chris Lanier, Jesse Reklaw and John Isaacson
for their advice and assistance.

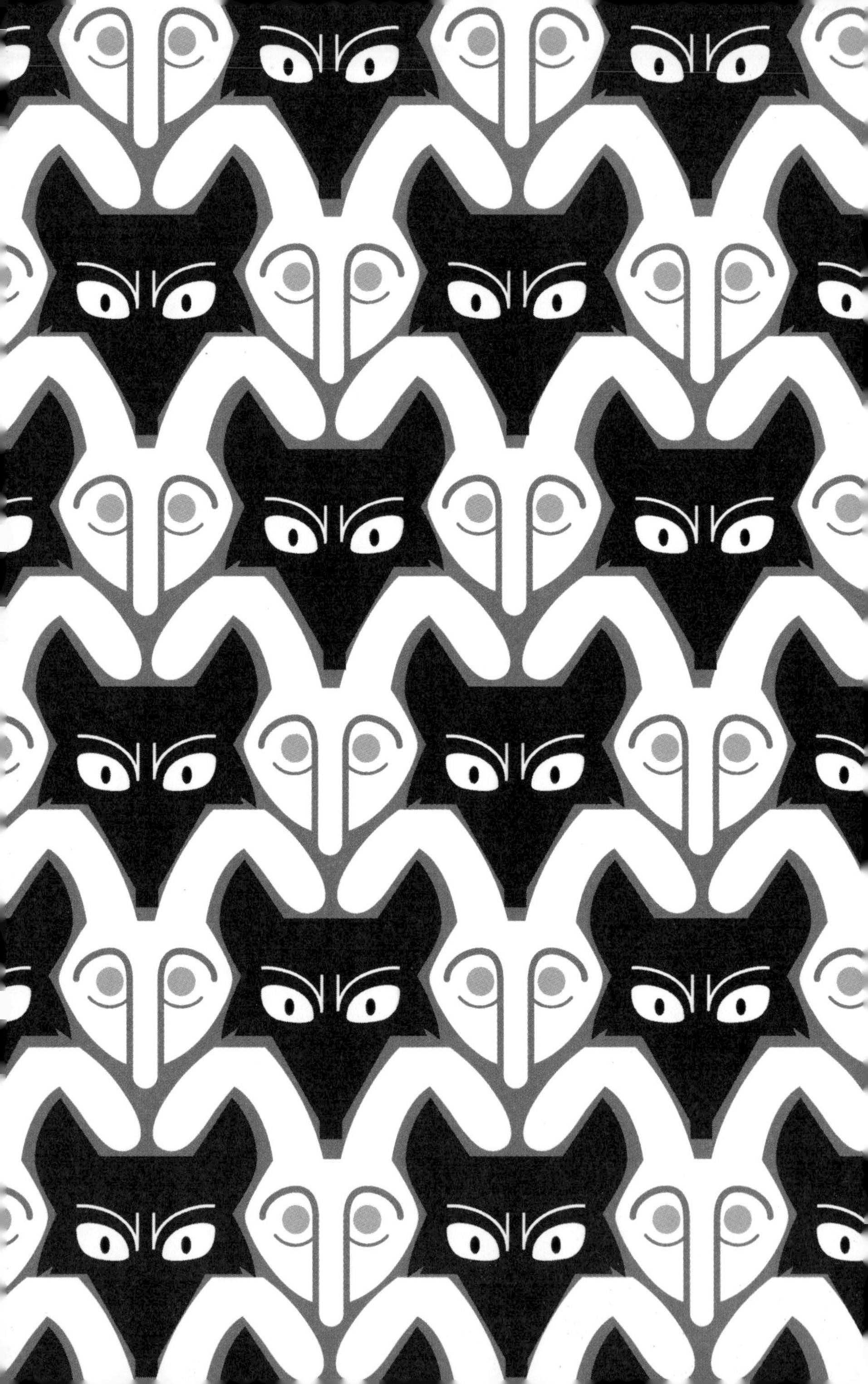